Beyond
Grapes

Recipes for Amazing Homemade Wines and Liqueurs Made from (Almost) Anything but Grapes

Yacov Morad

Pomegranate Wine

LIBRARY TALES PUBLISHING
WWW.LIBRARYTALESPUBLISHING.COM

For general information on our other products and services, please contact our Customer Care Department at 1-800-754-5016. For technical support, please visit WWW.LIBRARYTALESPUBLISHING.COM

Library Tales Publishing also publishes its books in a variety of electronic formats. Every content that appears in print is available in electronic books.

*** PRINTED IN THE UNITED STATES OF AMERICA ***

978-1956769753

Cinnamon Liqueur

Table of Contents

FRUIT WINE RECIPES

VEGETABLE WINES

MEDICINAL HERB WINES

LIQUEURS

DRIED FRUIT LIQUEURS

MEDICINAL PLANT LIQUEURS

Chocolate Liqueur

Foreword

At the tender age of 10, I watched my father make wine on a small plot of land just outside our home. By the age of 12, I was making wine all by myself and dreaming of one day having a winery of my own. In 1968, while on a trip to Mount Hermon (the only snowcapped mountain in Israel), I met my future wife—the love of my life, Ester. When I shared my winemaking dreams with her, she told me that her father also made wine as a hobby. When I visited my future in-laws for the very first time, I was greeted by the scent of fermentation and the sight of jars and bottles filled with liquids of assorted colors. Ester's father opened a bottle of white wine and poured out two glasses. He handed me a glass, and we toasted "L'chaim." The wine was excellent but strange. It didn't taste like any other wine I'd ever had.

"What kind of wine is this?" I asked.

"Pumpkin," he answered with a smile. "Pumpkin wine!"

To my delighted surprise, Ester's father had a large cellar filled with wines made from a variety of fruits and vegetables: pomegranates, apples, carrots, and beets, as well as grapes. Having discovered a new kind of wine, I completely fell in love with the idea of making unusual and exotic wines. The minute I got back home, I began studying, brewing, fermenting, and making my own wine from a wide assortment of fruits, vegetables, and medicinal herbs. I tried everything from passionfruit to lychee, pomegranates, strawberries, parsley, dates, watermelon, sage, and much, much more.

After 30 years of experience, I decided to convert my lifelong hobby into a profession. I opened my very own winery in 1999, and since then, Morad Winery has been a household name in Israel (the first commercial winery in Israel to make wine out of almost anything BUT grapes). I've appeared on many popular TV shows and news broadcasts and hosted hundreds of thousands of visitors from all around the world in the winery's visitor's center. It's 20 years later, and I'm still married to my wonderful wife, Ester. Although we have both retired from the day-to-day operations of the winery, we are still making wine. However, our focus has changed. We now spend most of our time teaching students from all around the world how to make delicious wine from almost anything BUT grapes, in the comfort of their own homes. Now, I would like to impart that knowledge, comprised of a lifetime of winemaking experience, to you.

I have written this book with the hope of inspiring within you the same kind of excitement that I had when I was first introduced to this new world of wine. I wanted to challenge the notion that wine is made only from grapes and inspire a new generation of winemakers to make a new kind of wine. I can say with confidence that specialty wine proved to be not only a great hobby and a challenging profession but also a constant, never-ending source of inspiration.

To this day, more than 10 years after retiring from my business, I am still discovering new and exciting flavors. I'm still making wine, and I'm still fascinated by new developments, new wine possibilities, and the endless combinations of flavors. I'm still developing new wines, new recipes, and new formulas to make the process easier for newcomers and pros alike. I hope you enjoy this book and find that it delivered on the promise it made.

Yacov Morad

Date Wine

INTRODUCTION

If you think that all fine wines start on a grapevine, you are in for a delightful, eye-opening treat. What you will discover in this book are recipes, developed over many years of creative experimentation, for making distinctive wines and liqueurs from fruits, vegetables, and medicinal herbs. These recipes will guide you through the process of making versatile and vibrant specialty wines in the comfort of your own home. Wines and liqueurs to share with family and friends at informal events and for those memorable, once-in-a-lifetime occasions.

Today, there are many fine wines made from grapes grown at prestigious wineries all over the world. But alongside the fancy mass-production of wine, there has always been the unassuming practice of homemade winemaking. This book of wine recipes that you are now holding in your hands falls into the old and venerable tradition of homemade winemaking, with a twist. It isn't about making wine from grapes but about making wines and liqueurs from almost anything but grapes: from fruits and vegetables to spices and herbs.

This is a hobby you can indulge in at any time of year, whether it's a cup of chocolate liqueur on Christmas Eve or a glass of watermelon wine on a hot summer day.

<u>Wine vs. Liqueur</u>

Wine is traditionally made from fermented grapes, while fruit wines and specialty wines can be produced from anything BUT grapes. The winemaking process involves fermentation (anything that has sugar in it can technically ferment, and therefore be made into wine) and requires aging, which might take several months, depending on the type of wine you choose to make.

On the other hand, liqueurs (not to be confused with liquors) are sweetened alcoholic beverages that are made by soaking fruits, vegetables, or medicinal herbs in alcohol. We "extract" the flavor, add sugar, and serve cold. They are quick and easy to make and have a higher alcoholic content.

UTENSILS, TOOLS, APPLIANCES, AND INGREDIENTS NEEDED FOR WINEMAKING

The first step in the process of making any one of the specialty wine recipes included in this book is to gather all the necessary items. This includes containers, lids, utensils, appliances, tools, general winemaking ingredients, and any specialty food ingredients required for the specific recipe you are following.

All the necessary utensils and tools can be bought at any store that sells winemaking equipment, or you can find them online.

For starters, you will need two containers:

(1) THE PREPARATION CONTAINER
The preparation container must be suitable for food use. It can be made of glass, plastic, or metal. This container must be large enough to hold at least twice as much as the fermentation container since it will have to hold all the fruit and other ingredients used in the first fermentation. It will also be needed for transferring the brew from one container to another.

(2) FERMENTATION CONTAINER
For best results, the fermentation container should be made of glass and be large enough to accommodate all the ingredients used in the fermentation process. It should also have a narrow nozzle. The container should be transparent because it is important for you to see what is happening during the fermentation process. For example, you will want to monitor the sediment that forms at the bottom of the container and the fermentation process before and after adding sorbate.

Both containers must be cleaned and then sanitized with boiling hot water prior to use to ensure a bacteria-free environment.

(4) A LID FOR THE FERMENTATION CONTAINER

The lid for the fermentation container must fit tightly and have a hole in its center to accommodate the airlock. You can purchase "Fermentation Lids" on Amazon for as little as $10, or buy a sealed fermentation container that comes with a pre-installed lid.

(5) AN AIRLOCK

The airlock is a bent pipe resembling a siphon. It is used to seal the fermentation container, preventing air from getting in while allowing air to go out.

(6) A LARGE SIEVE

The sieve is needed to filter out the fruit.

(7) A LARGE FUNNEL

The funnel is used to pour the liquid from the preparation container into the fermentation container during the draining process.

(8) A DRAINAGE SIPHON / SIPHON PUMP

The drainage siphon is used for siphoning and transferring liquid from one container to another.

(9) A PITCHER FOR POURING

(10) A LARGE GARBAGE BAG OR OTHER RECEPTACLE FOR FRUIT AND VEGETABLE RESIDUE.

(11) A THICK CLOTH TO COVER CONTAINERS

Straining cloth (you could use the same cloth as the container cover, but we recommend you use a separate cloth to strain).

(12) WINE BOTTLES AND CORKS
(13) A LARGE POT
(14) FOOD PROCESSOR OR BLENDER
(15) MEASURING CUP / MEASURING SPOON SET

MAKING THE WINE YEAST

Yeast is a single-cell, microscopic fungus that is fed by the sugars in a brew. Yeast eats, produces energy and by-products, and multiplies. If it is not nourished by sugar, yeast decomposes into starch.

Yeast works in two different environments: either in an aerobic one where oxygen is present, or in an anaerobic environment where only a very small amount or no oxygen is present. During the aerobic activity of yeast, called "breathing," yeast produces a lot of energy, emits carbon dioxide and water, and multiplies. In yeast anaerobic activity, the yeast produces very little energy, emits very little carbon dioxide, and produces various forms of alcohol and acids. In this kind of yeast activity, the level of yeast reproduction is small and fermentation occurs. So, the winemaking process requires yeast preparation to produce an anaerobic yeast environment.

Each wine recipe will use 0.2 grams of prepared wine yeast per 1 liter (33.814 ounces) of liquid.

Preparation of the Wine Yeast
(Per 1 liter / 0.264 gallons)

You will need:

- Warm water
- Sugar
- A clean measuring cup
- A thick cloth or cheesecloth

Heat 60 ml of water until warm (not hot) and pour it into a clean glass cup. Add 1 teaspoon of sugar to the cup of warm water. Mix until the sugar is completely dissolved. Cover with a thick cloth and let it sit to cool.

When the glass is cool to the touch (below 30°C), add 0.2 grams of yeast per liter. Cover the cup with a thick cloth and place it at room temperature in a place that's warm but not hot, making sure to avoid direct sunlight.

During this time, the yeast will become "active." After 20-30 minutes of activity, the yeast is ready to be added to the brew.

Feeding the Wine Yeast
To prolong fermentation, wine yeast must be provided with several essential nutrients, listed and described below. Which nutrients are to be added, and when, are noted in each recipe. So please be sure to reference the following pages as you make your wine:

Ammonium Phosphate

This provides yeast with both nitrogen and phosphorus.

Amount to be used: 1 gram per liter.

To add to the brew: First, remove a small amount of brew from the container and put it into a pitcher. Add the noted amount of ammonium phosphate to the brew in the pitcher, mix well, and pour the mixture back into the container. The "required amount" will be specified for each recipe.

Citric Acid

Wine yeast requires an acidic environment to thrive and reproduce. Citric acid provides such an environment while enriching the flavor of the brew. It also kills unwanted bacteria and keeps the wine healthy.

Amount to be used: 1 gram per liter.

To add to the brew: First, remove a small amount of the brew from the container and put it into a pitcher. Add the required amount of citric acid to the brew in the pitcher, mix well, and pour the mixture back into the container.

Sulfite

Potassium metabisulfite is a preservative that prevents the decomposition of the fruits or vegetables used. However, it is important to add a precise amount of sulfite, since too much of it could damage the yeast and impair both the taste and color of your wine. An excessive amount is also dangerous to your health!

Amount to be used: 0.2 gram per liter

To add to the brew: First, remove a small amount of the brew from the container and put it into a pitcher. Add the required amount of sulfite to the brew in the pitcher, mix well, and pour the mixture back into the container.

Warning: Keep sulfite out of the reach of children!

Bentonite

This is a naturally extracted mineral. Its tiny flakes separate to cover a large surface area when added to water, becoming a uniform slurry. When put into wine, bentonite absorbs any undesirable particles in the brew and drags them to the bottom of the container, creating a visible sediment that is easy to filter out.

Amount to be used: 1 gram per liter. For every 1 liter, add 50 ml of water and bentonite. The amount of water should be 10 times greater than the amount of bentonite.

To add to the brew: In a small pitcher, add 10 ml of water and 1 gram of bentonite. Stir for a few minutes (FYI, the mixture may stick to your spoon). Leave the spoon in the pitcher. Cover the pitcher with a piece of cloth and put it aside for a day. On the second day, add 5 ml of water, mix again, and re-cover. On the third day, mix again. This time the mixture should be less thick. Mix a little bit of the brew into the pitcher and pour everything back into the container.

Sorbate

Potassium sorbate slows down oxidation, works against the buildup of mold, and stops the yeast from overgrowing, thus preventing or hindering changes to the color or taste of food. It is often added to wine as well as to food products.

Amount to be used: 0.2 grams per 1 liter of brew.

To add to the brew: After aging, and just before putting the brew into wine bottles, add sorbate to the brew to prevent the growth of fungi and mold, and to maintain the wine's color. First, remove a small amount of the brew from the container and put it into a pitcher. Add the required amount of sorbate to the brew in the pitcher, mix well, and pour the mixture back into the container.

Warning: Keep sorbate out of the reach of children!

THE WINEMAKING PROCESS

So, let's begin! This is an overall review of the winemaking process, and while each recipe will guide you through the step-by-step process, it should be noted that an understanding of this process will help you get a leg-up as you dive into the individual recipes.

Step 1: Preparing Wine Yeast

The first thing that needs to be done is to prepare the wine yeast (see p. 14 for instructions). While the wine yeast is cooling, proceed to Step 2.

Step 2: Making the Unfermented Brew

For this part of the process, you will need to prepare the Fermentation Container. Here's what you need:

> A glass container with a fermentation stopper and airlock
> A large funnel
> A large sieve
> A pitcher for pouring
> A large garbage bag
> 30 milliliters of water

Boil the water, let it cool to 30°C, add yeast, and allow it to ferment.

****

Boil water and add sugar to it, stirring the water until the sugar completely dissolves. Put the base (fruit, vegetable, etc.) into the preparation container and pour the boiled sugared water over it. Cover the preparation container with a thick cloth and set it aside to cool. When the unfermented brew is cool, add the ammonium phosphate and prepared wine yeast. Cover with a piece of cloth (cheesecloth is recommended) and let it rest for X days (each recipe needs a different amount of time), stirring it twice each day for the X days.

After X days, skim off any material floating on the surface of the brew. Remove the fruit from the brew using the sieve for straining. Lightly strain out as much of the juice as possible with your hands. Put the fruit residue in a large garbage bag (or other receptacle). Then transfer only the liquid from the preparation container into the fermentation container. Close the fermentation container with the lid and airlock.

At this point, alcoholic anaerobic fermentation starts. The yeast now breaks down the sugars into alcohol and CO_2, which are emitted through the airlock. The fermentation will last about 12 days, gradually subsiding. You will know the fermentation process has ended when there are no more bubbles coming up through the airlock. Once the fermentation stops, add sulfite (see instructions on p. 15 for adding sulfite to the brew).

Once movement inside the fermentation container calms down, the process of sedimentation begins. Even after you have filtered out most of the fruit, many tiny food particles remain floating about in the brew. These particles now sink to the bottom of the container and the liquid starts to clear. When the brew is reasonably clear, it is ready for draining.

Draining

When fermentation is complete, it's time to extract the clear liquid from the brew. You can drain the clear liquid from the fermentation container with a plastic tube, a hose, or a fish tank drainer. Draw off only the clear liquid, leaving the sediment at the bottom of the fermentation container. Pour the clear liquid into a clean preparatory container. Wash the fermentation container, rinsing away all the leftover sediment. Pump all the clear liquid now in the preparatory container back into the fermentation container. If the wine is not clear enough, clarify it with bentonite. See instructions on page 5 for adding bentonite to the brew.

Close the fermentation container with the fermentation stopper. Put the fermentation container containing the wine in a cool, dark place to age.

After aging, but just before bottling the wine, add sorbate to protect against fungal and mold growth, and to maintain the wine's color. See instructions on page 6 for adding sorbate to the wine.

Summary

Prepare the wine yeast 20 to 30 minutes before putting it into the brew. The location of the fermentation container during aging is extremely important. In a warm place, yeast works faster, and sugar is depleted. In a cool place, fermentation is slower, so it is recommended that you always place the fermentation container in a cool, dark place for aging.

Do not put the fermentation container in a completely sealed room. The room where you leave the fermentation container to age must have an open window to allow the gas emissions that occur during fermentation to leave the room and fresh air to come in. Make sure the container is not exposed to the sun. Sunlight is the enemy!

When fermenting wines, after the first fermentation and draining are finished, check the taste of the wine to decide how to proceed. If the wine is too sweet, continue to ferment but do not add more sugar. If the wine is dry or lacks flavor, add sugar (sweetening restores the flavor). In all cases, continue fermentation until aging is completed.

In some fermented wines, an overflowing of the fruit can occur, either with or without foaming. So you need to pay close attention to what's happening. It is recommended that you put the fermentation container in a sink in case it overflows.

Fruit Wines

Fruit wines can be made from whole fresh fruit, crushed fresh fruit, or freshly squeezed or bottled fruit juices.

Raspberry Wine

Ingredients
(for making 1 Liter of wine)

- 600 grams of ripe raspberries
- 30 grams of dark raisins
- 400 ml boiled and cooled water
- 350 grams of sugar
- 1 gram of Ammonium phosphate
- 1 gram of citric acid
- 0.2 grams of prepared yeast
- 0.2 grams of sulfite
- 0.2 grams of sorbate

> **1 Liter = 0.264 Gallon**
> **1 Gram = 0.035 Ounces**
> **1 ml = 0.033 oz**

The Process

(1) Put 600 grams of ripe raspberries into a preparation container. Add 200 grams of sugar and cover with a thick cloth or cheesecloth. Let sit for 24 hours.

(2) Wash and cut 30 grams of dark raisins and add them to the container. Add 200 ml of water. Add 1 gram of ammonium phosphate. Add 1 gram of citric acid and the prepared yeast. Mix well and cover the container with cheesecloth. Let sit for 5 days. Each day mix well to remove the foam.

(3) Gently strain and filter the brew into the fermentation container.

(4) Add 200 ml of water and 150 grams of sugar to the mix. Close the container with a fermentation stopper and let sit for 7 days.

(5) When fermentation weakens or stops, add 0.2 grams of sulfite and close with a fermentation stopper.

(6) 10 days after the fermentation is complete, drain the clear liquid and age for 4 months.

(7) Just before putting the brew into wine bottles add 0.2 grams of sorbate per liter to protect the color and flavor of the wine.

Prickly Pear

Ingredients
(for making 1 Liter of wine)

- 900 grams of ripe, peeled sabers (watch out for spikes!)
- 200 ml of water
- 300 grams of sugar
- 1 gram of citric acid
- 1 gram of ammonium phosphate
- 0.2 grams of prepared yeast
- 0.2 grams of sulfite
- 0.2 grams of sorbate

The Process

(1) Cut 900 grams of sabers into small cubes and place in a clean, sanitized container. Add 200 grams of sugar and mix lightly. Cover the container with cheesecloth and transfer to a cool, dark place. Let sit for 48 hours.

(2) Add 100 ml of water, the citric acid, the ammonium phosphate, and the prepared yeast. Mix well. Cover the container with cheesecloth and let sit for 5 days in a cool, dark place.

(3) Strain and filter into a clean container, then add 100 ml of water and close with fermentation stopper. Let sit for 12 days in a cool, dark place.

(4) When fermentation slows, add 0.2 grams of sulfite. Drain as needed and age 5 months in a cool, dark place.

(5) Before bottling, add 0.2 grams of sorbate.

Citron Wine

Ingredients
(for making 1 Liter of wine)

• 900 ml of water
• 500 grams of citrons (peeled)
• 50 grams of citrons (unpeeled)
• 300 grams of sugar
• 1 gram of citric acid
• 1 gram of ammonium phosphate
• 0.2 grams of prepared yeast
• 0.2 grams of sulfite
• 0.2 grams of sorbate

The Process

(1) Cut 500 grams of peeled citrons into thin disc-shape slices and put into a preparation container. Add the unpeeled citrons. Sprinkle 150 grams of sugar on top of the fruit and cover the container. Let sit in a cool, dark place for 24 hours.

(2) After 24 hours gently strain the fruit and filter the liquid into the fermentation container.

(3) Add 900 ml of lukewarm water and 150 grams of sugar. Add the prepared yeast, the citric acid and ammonium phosphate. Close the container with a fermentation stopper. Let it ferment for 7 days in a cool, dark place.

(4) After 7 days the fermentation will weaken. Add the sulfite to stop the fermentation. After another 10 days, drain until the liquid is clear. Age 4 months in a cool, dark place.

(5) Before bottling, add 0.2 grams of sorbate to protect the color and flavor of the wine.

Sapodilla Wine

Ingredients
(for making 1 Liter of wine)

- 400 grams of peeled sapodillas
- 300 grams of sugar
- 550 ml of water
- 1 gram of citric acid
- 1 gram of phosphate
- 0.2 grams of prepared yeast
- 0.2 grams of sulfite
- 0.2 grams of sorbate

The Process

(1) Put 400 grams of peeled sapodillas into a preparation container. Add 150 grams of sugar, 350 ml of water but do not mix. Add 1 gram of citric acid, 1 gram of phosphate, and the prepared yeast. Cover the container with a cloth and let sit for 5 days in a cool, dark place.

(2) Strain the fruit and filter the liquid into a fermentation container. Heat 200 ml of water, add 150 grams of sugar to the water and mix. Let the mixture cool down.

(3) Add brew to the fermentation container and close with a fermentation stopper. Let sit in a cool, dark place for 7 days.

(4) After 7 days stop the fermentation by adding 0.2 grams of sulfite.

(5) 7 days after fermentation has stopped, drain. Move the container to a cool, dark place and age 4 months.

(6) Before bottling, add 0.2 grams of sorbate per liter to protect the color and flavor of the wine.

Date Wine

Ingredients
(for making 1 Liter of wine)

• 450 grams of sweet dates
• 800 ml of water
• 400 grams of sugar
• 1 gram of citric acid
• 1 gram of ammonium phosphate
• 0.2 grams of prepared yeast
• 0.2 grams of sulfite
• 0.2 grams of sorbate

The Process

(1) Put the dates into a preparation container. In a separate container, heat 600 ml of water. Add 200 grams of sugar and stir until the sugar dissolves. Pour the sugar water over the dates and let cool for 4 hours.

(2) Add the citric acid, ammonium phosphate, and prepared yeast. Stir and cover the container with cheesecloth. Let it rest for 5 days in a cool, dark place.

(3) After 5 Days Strain the fruit and filter the liquid into a fermentation container. Add 200 ml of water and 200 grams of sugar. Close the container with a fermentation stopper and allow it to ferment for 7 days in a cool, dark place.

(4) When fermentation subsides, add 0.2 grams of sulfite to stop fermentation. 10 days after fermentation stops, drain. Age 6 months in a cool, dark place.

(5) Before bottling, add 0.2 grams of sorbate per liter to protect the color and flavor of the wine.

Grapefruit Wine

Ingredients
(for making 1 Liter of wine)

• 700 grams of peeled grapefruit
• 400 grams of sugar
• 300 ml of freshly squeezed grapefruit juice
• 1 gram of citric acid
• 1 gram of ammonium phosphate
• 0.2 grams of prepared yeast
• 0.2 grams of sulfite
• 0.2 grams of sorbate

The Process

(1) Peel and chop 700 grams of grapefruit and place in a preparation container. Sprinkle 200 grams of sugar on the grapefruit and cover with a thick cloth or cheesecloth. Let sit for 5 hours.

(2) After 5 hours, strain the fruit and filter the liquid into a fermentation tank.

(3) Add 300 ml of freshly squeezed grapefruit juice and 200 grams of sugar. Add the citric acid, ammonium phosphate, and prepared yeast. Close the container with a fermentation stopper and let it sit for 5 days in a cool, dark place.

(4) After 5 days Once the fermentation has stopped or weakened, add 0.2 grams of sulfite and let sit for 30 days in a cool, dark place.

(5) After 30 days have passed, drain and age 4 months. Before bottling, add 0.2 grams of sorbate.

Mandarin Wine

Ingredients
(for making 1 Liter of wine)

- 500 grams of chopped mandarins
- 400 ml of mandarin juice
- 400 grams of sugar
- 1 gram of ammonium phosphate
- 0.2 grams of prepared yeast
- 0.2 grams of sulfite
- 0.2 grams of sorbate

*1 kg of tangerines produces
580 ml of juice.*

The Process

(1) Chop and peel the 500 grams of mandarins and put into a preparation container. Sprinkle 200 grams of sugar over the mandarins and add 200 ml of the mandarin juice. Cover the container with a thick cloth or cheesecloth and let sit for 24 hours in a cool, dark place.

(2) After 24 hours, strain and filter, add 200 ml of freshly squeezed mandarin juice and 200 grams of sugar. Stir until the sugar completely dissolves.

(3) Add the ammonium phosphate and prepared yeast. Close the container with a fermentation stopper and let it rest for 7 days.

(4) After 7 days, add 0.2 grams of sulfite and let rest for another 10 days. Drain and age for 3 months in a cool, dark pace.

(5) Before bottling, add 0.2 grams of sorbate.

Cherry Wine

Ingredients
(for making 1 Liter of wine)

• 500 grams of ripe cherries
(with the pit)
• 500 ml of water
• 450 grams of sugar
• 1 gram of ammonium phosphate
• 1 gram of citric acid
• 0.2 grams of prepared yeast
• 0.2 grams of sulfite
• 0.2 grams of sorbate

* Cherry wine is best served cold.

The Process

(1) Put the 500 grams of cherries into a preparation container, sprinkle 200 grams of sugar over the fruit and cover the container with cheesecloth. Let it sit for 5 hours in a cool, dark place.

(2) Add 300 ml of water, the prepared yeast, the citric acid and the ammonium phosphate to the container. Cover the container with a thick cloth and let sit for 5 days in a cool, dark place.

(3) After 5 days, strain and filter the brew into a fermentation container using a funnel and strainer. Meanwhile, in a pot, heat 200 ml of the water. Add and dissolve 250 grams of sugar in the water. Refrigerate the sugar water for 30 minutes and add to the fermentation container. Close the container with a fermentation stopper and let it ferment for 7 days in a cool, dark place.

(4) After 7 days, stop the fermentation by adding 0.2 grams of sulfite. Re-seal the container and let sit for 10 days. After 10 days, when you are sure the fermentation has stopped, drain. Rinse the fermentation container and return the clear liquid to it. Close the container with a fermentation stopper. Age in a cool, dark place for 4 months.

(5) Before bottling, add 0.2 grams of sorbate.

Guava Wine

Ingredients
(for making 1 Liter of wine)

- 400 grams of raspberry guava
- 500 ml of water
- 300 grams of sugar
- 1 gram of citric acid.
- 1 gram of ammonium phosphate
- 0.2 grams of prepared yeast
- 0.2 grams of sulfite
- 0.2 grams of sorbate

The Process

(1) Peel and cut the 400 grams of guava and place in a preparation container. Sprinkle 100 grams of sugar over the fruit. Cover the container with dense cloth and let sit for 3 days in a cool, dark place.

(2) Add 300 ml of the water, the ammonium phosphate, the citric acid, and the prepared yeast. Lightly stir the mixture, then cover the container with cheesecloth and let sit for 3 days in a cool, dark place. Strain the liquid into the fermentation container.

(3) In a pot, heat 200 ml of the water on low heat and dissolve 200 grams of sugar in the water. Refrigerate for 30 minutes then add it to the fermentation container. Close the container with a fermentation stopper and let sit for 7 days in a cool, dark place.

(4) Once fermentation subsides, add 0.2 grams of sulfite and re-seal the container with the fermentation stopper.

(5) 10 days after fermentation stops, drain. Seal the container again with the fermentation stopper. Drain again as needed. Once the brew is clear, age 4 months in a cool, dark place.

(6) Before bottling, add 0.2 grams of sorbate per liter.

Apricot Wine

Ingredients
(for making 1 Liter of wine)

- 650 grams of ripe, pitted apricots
- 700 ml of water
- 450 grams of sugar
- 1 gram of citric acid
- 1 gram of ammonium phosphate
- 0.2 grams of prepared yeast
- 0.2 grams of sulfite
- 0.2 grams of sorbate

The Process

(1) Cut the 650 grams of pitted apricots into small pieces and put into a preparation container. Sprinkle 200 grams of sugar over the fruit and cover the container with a thick cloth or cheesecloth. Let sit for 24 hours in a cool, dark place.

(2) After 24 hours, add to the preparation container 450 ml of water, the prepared yeast, the citric acid, and the ammonium phosphate. Cover with a cloth and let it sit for 5 days. After 5 days, filter the liquid into the fermentation container with a funnel and strainer.

(3) In a pot, heat 250 ml of the water and dissolve 250 grams of sugar in it. Refrigerate for 30 minutes, then add to the fermentation container and close the container with a fermentation stopper. Let it sit for 7 days in a cool, dark place.

(4) Taste the brew for sweetness. If it's to your liking, add 0.2 grams of sulfite and re-seal the container with a fermentation stopper. Two weeks after fermentation ends, drain and age 4 months in a cool, dark place.

(5) Before bottling, add 0.2 grams of sorbate per liter.

Rice Wine

Ingredients
(for making 1 Liter of wine)

- 120 grams of basmati rice
- 50 grams of golden raisins
- 1600 ml of water
- 400 grams of sugar
- 1 gram of citric acid
- 0.2 grams of prepared yeast
- 0.2 grams of sulfite
- 0.2 grams of sorbate

The Process

(1) Cook 120 grams of basmati rice in 1,600 ml of water over low heat until the rice softens and leave to cool. Make sure the rice isn't too soft. There should still be 800 ml of liquid in the pot (if missing, add water).

(2) Strain and filter the remaining liquid into a new pot. Add 400 grams of sugar, add the raisins and mix well, let cool.

(3) Transfer the brew to the fermentation tank. Add the ammonium phosphate, citric acid, and the prepared yeast to the container. Cover with a thick cloth and let sit for 5 days.

(4) After 5 days, strain the raisins and sediment out and transfer the clear brew back to the fermentation tank. Close the container with a fermentation stopper and let sit for 10 days in a cool, dark place.

(5) Stop the fermentation process by adding 0.2 g of sulfite. Drain and leave to age for 6 months.

(6) Before bottling, add 0.2 grams of sorbate.

Marula Wine

Ingredients
(for making 1 Liter of wine)

- 800 grams of marula fruit
- 600 ml of water
- 400 grams of sugar
- 1 gram of citric acid
- 1 gram of ammonium phosphate
- 0.2 grams of prepared yeast
- 0.2 grams of sulfite
- 0.2 grams of sorbate

The Process

(1) Peel the 800 grams of marulas and add to the preparation container, along with any extracted juice. Add 100 grams of sugar and cover the container with a thick cloth or cheesecloth. Let sit for 6 hours.

(2) In a pot, add 100 grams of sugar to 400 ml of water, heat until the sugar has completely dissolved. Then add the ammonium phosphate, the citric acid, and the prepared yeast to the container. Cover the container with a thick cloth. Let sit for 5 days.

(3) Strain and filter into a fermentation container. Heat 200 ml of the water in a pot and stir in 200 grams of sugar, keep stirring until the sugar is completely dissolved. Let the sugar water cool down, then add to the fermentation container. Close the container with a fermentation stopper and let sit for 7 days in a cool, dark place.

(4) Once fermentation is complete, add 0.2 grams of sulfite to the brew and re-seal the container. 10 days after fermentation is finished, drain.

(5) Allow the wine to age 5 months in a cool, dark place.

(6) Before bottling, add 0.2 grams of sorbate per liter.

Kiwi Wine

Ingredients
(for making 1 Liter of wine)

• 800 grams of kiwi (peeled)
• 600 ml of water
• 400 grams of sugar
• 1 gram of citric acid
• 1 gram of ammonium phosphate
• 0.2 grams of prepared yeast
• 0.2 grams of sulfite
• 0.2 grams of sorbate

The Process

(1) Heat 300 ml of water and pour into a small container, dissolve 200 grams of sugar and refrigerate for 30 minutes.

(2) Peel 800 grams of kiwi and cut each piece of fruit in 2, add to brew.

(3) Add 1 gram of citric acid, 1 gram of ammonium phosphate, and prepared yeast. Mix and cover in a dense cloth for 5 days.

(4) After 5 days, add 200 grams of sugar to 300 ml of water in a separate container. Stir until the sugar dissolves and let cool.

(5) Strain and filter the contents of the fermentation preparation container. Add the cooled sugar water, close with fermentation stopper for 7 days to add 0.2 grams of sulfite.

(6) When the fermentation stops, drain. Age for 5 months.

(7) Before bottling, add 0.2 grams of sorbate per liter. Serve cold.

Annona Wine

Ingredients
(for making 1 Liter of wine)

- 800 grams of annona (with the peel)
- 600 ml of water
- 400 grams of sugar
- 1 gram of citric acid
- 1 gram of ammonium phosphate
- 0.2 grams of prepared yeast
- 0.2 grams of sulfite
- 0.2 grams of sorbate

The Process

(1) Dissolve 200 grams of the sugar in 400 ml of hot (not boiling) water. Cut each of the annonas in half and put into a preparation container. Pour the sugar water over the fruit and let cool.

(2) Add 1 gram of citric acid, 1 gram of ammonium phosphate, and the prepared yeast. Cover the container with a thick cloth and let sit for 5 days.

(3) Dissolve the remaining 200 grams of sugar in 200 ml of hot (not boiling) water and allow to cool. Strain and filter into the fermentation container. Add the sugar-water and close the fermentation container with a fermentation stopper. Let sit for 7 days.

(4) When the fermentation has stopped, add 0.2 grams of sulfite to the brew. Let sit for 10 days, then drain.

(5) Age 3 months in a cool, dark place.

(6) Before bottling, add 0.2 grams of sorbate per liter.

Jackfruit Wine

Ingredients
(for making 1 Liter of wine)

- 500 grams of jackfruit, peeled
- 500 ml of water
- 400 grams of sugar
- 1 gram of citric acid
- 1 gram of ammonium phosphate
- 0.2 grams of prepared yeast
- 0.2 grams of sulfite
- 0.2 grams of sorbate

The Process

(1) Cut each of the 500 grams of peeled jackfruit in half, extract its contents and transfer into a preparation container, add 200 grams of sugar and cover the container with a thick cloth. Let sit for 5 hours.

(2) After 5 hours add 300 ml of water, the ammonium phosphate, the citric acid, and the prepared yeast. Mix lightly and re-cover the container with the thick cloth. Let sit for another 5 days. Strain the liquid into a fermentation container.

(3) Heat 200 ml of water and dissolve 200 grams of sugar in it. Let cool and then close the container with a fermentation stopper. Let sit for 7 days in a cool, dark place. Once fermentation subsides add 0.2 grams of sulfite and re-seal the container with a fermentation stopper.

(4) 10 days after the fermentation stops, drain and close the container again with a fermentation stopper. If necessary, drain again until the liquid is clear. Once the liquid has cleared, age 4 months in a cool, dark place.

(5) Before bottling, add 0.2 grams of sorbate per liter.

Plum Wine

Ingredients
(for making 1 Liter of wine)

• 800 ml of drained plum juice
• 100 grams of dark raisins, cut into small pieces
• 300 grams of sugar
• 1 gram of citric acid
• 1 gram of ammonium phosphate
• 0.2 grams of prepared yeast
• 0.2 grams of sulfite
• 0.2 grams of sorbate

The Process

(1) Put the 800 ml of squeezed plum juice into a preparation container. Add the 100 grams of cut up raisins and 300 grams of sugar. Stir, then add 1 gram of citric acid, 1 gram of ammonium phosphate, and the prepared yeast.

(2) Close the container with a fermentation stopper and let sit for 7 days.

(3) Once fermentation subsides, and air bubble activity has ceased, add 0.2 grams of sulfite to stop the fermentation. Let sit for 10 days in a cool, dark place.

(4) Drain and close the container again with the fermentation stopper. Age 6 months in a cool, dark place.

(5) Before bottling, add 0.2 grams of sorbate per liter.

Cranberry Wine

Ingredients
(for making 1 Liter of wine)

- 500 grams of cranberries
- 800 ml of water
- 350 grams of sugar
- 0.2 grams of prepared yeast
- 1 gram of ammonium phosphate
- 1 gram of citric acid
- 0.2 grams of sulfite
- 0.2 grams of sorbate

The Process

(1) Put the 500 grams of cranberries into a preparation container and crush them (you can use a nylon straining bag). Sprinkle 200 grams of sugar on top of the crushed fruit and cover the container with a thick cloth. Let sit for 4 hours.

(2) Add 400 ml of water, 1 gram of ammonium phosphate, 1 gram of citric acid, and the prepared yeast. Re-cover with the thick cloth and let sit for 5 days.

(3) Strain everything through a funnel and filter into a fermentation container. Add 400 ml of water and 150 grams of sugar to a separate pot. Mix well until the sugar is dissolved then add to the fermentation container.

(4) Close with a fermentation stopper and allow the brew to ferment for 7 days.

(5) After 7 days, stop the fermentation by adding 0.2 grams of sulfite. 10 days after the fermentation has stopped, drain. Age at least 3 months in a cool, dark place.

(6) Before bottling, add 0.2 grams of sorbate per liter.

Nectarine Wine

Ingredients
(for making 1 Liter of wine)

- 550 grams of nectarine, pitted
- 700 ml of water
- 400 grams of sugar
- 1 gram of citric acid
- 1 gram of ammonium phosphate
- 0.2 grams of prepared yeast
- 0.2 grams of sulfite
- 0.2 grams of sorbate

The Process

(1) Cut the 550 grams of nectarines (without the pits) into pieces and put into a preparation container.

(3) Dissolve 200 grams of sugar into 400 ml of water and add to the preparation container.

(4) Add 1 gram of citric acid, 1 gram of ammonium phosphate, and the prepared yeast. Cover the container with a thick cloth and let sit for 5 days.

(5) After 5 days, filter the brew into a fermentation container, add 300 ml of water and 200 grams of sugar. Close the fermentation container with a fermentation stopper and let sit for 7 days.

(6) Once fermentation has come to a stop, add 0.2 grams of sulfite. 10 days after stopping the fermentation, drain. Age 4 to 5 months in a cool, dark place.

(7) Before bottling, add 0.2 grams of sorbate per liter.

Banana Wine

Ingredients
(for making 1 Liter of wine)

- 350 grams of very ripe bananas
- 800 ml of water
- 360 grams of sugar
- 20 grams of lemon rind
- 20 grams of orange rind
- 20 ml of lemon juice
- 20 ml of orange juice
- 100 grams of golden raisins
- 1 gram of ammonium phosphate
- 1 gram of citric acid
- 0.2 grams of prepared yeast
- 0.2 grams of sulfite
- 0.2 grams of sorbate

The Process

(1) Cut the 350 grams of bananas into small pieces and put into a pot.

(2) Add 600 ml of water, 20 grams of lemon rind, and 20 grams of orange rind. Bring the water to a boil then cook for 10 minutes on low heat. Add 100 grams of golden raisins and mix. After you turn the heat off, cover the pot and let sit 4 hours to cool.

(3) Gently strain and filter into a preparation container. Add the yeast, 160 grams of sugar, and the ammonium phosphate. Cover the container with a thick cloth and let sit for 7 days.

(4) Filter into a fermentation container and add 200 ml of water and 200 grams of sugar. Allow the wine to ferment until no bubbles come up.

(5) Then add 0.2 grams of sulfite. 10 days after fermentation has completely stopped, drain.

(6) Age 5 months in a cool, dark place.

(7) Before bottling, add 0.2 grams of sorbate per liter.

Raisin Wine

Ingredients
(for making 1 Liter of wine)

- 150 grams of dark raisins
- 800 ml of water
- 400 grams of sugar
- 0.2 grams of prepared yeast
- 0.2 grams of sulfite
- 0.2 grams of sorbate
- 0.1 gram of ammonium phosphate

The Process

(1) Cut up the 150 grams of dark raisins into small pieces and put them into a clean and sanitized preparation container.

(2) Heat 600 ml of the water and dissolve 200 grams of sugar in it. Pour the warm sugar water over the raisins, cover the container with dense cloth and allow the mixture to cool for 4 hours. Then add the citric acid, ammonium phosphate, and the prepared yeast. Mix well, and cover the container with a thick cloth. Let sit for 5 days.

(3) Strain and filter into a fermentation container. Heat 200 ml of water, add 200 grams of sugar and mix until the sugar dissolves. Let cool then add to the fermentation container.

(4) Close the fermentation container with a fermentation stopper and let sit for 10 days.

(5) Once fermentation has slowed, add 0.2 grams of sulfite. 10 days after fermentation has completely stopped, drain. Drain again as needed until liquid is clear.

(6) Age 4 months in a cool, dark place.

(7) Before bottling, add 0.2 grams of sorbate.

Pear Wine

Ingredients
(for making 1 Liter of wine)

- 800 grams of ripe pears
- 700 ml of water
- 400 grams of sugar
- 0.2 grams of prepared yeast
- 1 gram of ammonium phosphate
- 1 gram of citric acid
- 0.2 grams of sulfite
- 0.2 grams of sorbate

The Process

(1) Cut each of the 800 grams of ripe pears in half and put into a preparation container (core included).

(2) Sprinkle 200 grams of sugar over the fruit in the container, then cover the container with a thick cloth and let sit for 24 hours.

(3) Then add 400 ml of water, 1 gram of ammonium phosphate, 1 gram of citric acid, and the prepared yeast. Stir and cover with a thick cloth, let it sit for 5 days.

(4) Strain and filter all the contents into a fermentation container. Heat 300 ml of water and add 200 grams of sugar. Stir until the sugar dissolves and let cool. After cooling, add the sugar water to the fermentation container and close with a fermentation stopper. Let sit for 7 days.

(5) Once fermentation has subsided, add 0.2 grams of sulfite and re-seal the container with a fermentation stopper. A week after fermentation has come to a stop, drain. Age 4 to 5 months in a cool, dark place.

(6) Before bottling, add 0.2 grams of sorbate per liter.

Strawberry Wine

Ingredients
(for making 1 Liter of wine)

- 400 grams of strawberries
- 400 ml of water
- 400 grams of sugar
- 0.2 grams of prepared yeast
- 1 gram of citric acid
- 1 gram of ammonium phosphate
- 0.2 grams of sulfite
- 0.2 grams of sorbate

The Process

(1) Cut the 400 grams of strawberries into pieces and put in a preparation container.

(2) Sprinkle 200 grams of sugar over the fruit and cover the container with a thick cloth. Let sit for 5 hours.

(3) After 5 days gently strain and filter into a fermentation container. Add 200 ml of water, 200 grams of sugar, 1 gram of citric acid, 1 gram of ammonium phosphate, and the prepared yeast.

(4) Close the fermentation container with a fermentation stopper and let sit for 7 days. Once fermentation has subsided, stop the fermentation by adding 0.2 grams of sulfite.

(5) 10 days after fermentation has stopped, drain. When the liquid is clear, close the fermentation container with a fermentation stopper and age 3 to 4 months in a cool, dark place.

(6) Before bottling add 0.2 grams of sorbate per liter

Surinam Cherry

Ingredients
(for making 1 Liter of wine)

- 500 grams of surinam cherries
- 80 grams of dark raisins
- 400 grams of sugar
- 650 ml of water
- 1 gram of citric acid
- 1 gram of ammonium phosphate
- 0.2 grams of prepared yeast
- 0.2 grams of sulfite
- 0.2 grams of sorbate

The Process

(1) Put the 500 grams of surinam cherries (without the pits) into a preparation container. Add 80 grams of dark raisins and 250 grams of sugar. Cover the container with a thick cloth and let sit for 48 hours.

(2) Add 500 ml of water, 1 gram of citric acid, 1 gram of ammonium phosphate, and the prepared yeast. Re-cover the container with the thick cloth and let sit for 5 days.

(3) After 5 days, strain and filter into a fermentation container. Heat 150 ml of water and add 150 grams of sugar to the water. Stir until the sugar is dissolved and let cool. Once cooled, add to the fermentation container and close the fermentation container with a fermentation stopper.

(4) Let sit for 7 days. After 7 days, stop fermentation with 0.2 grams of sulfite. 10 days after fermentation comes to a complete stop, drain. Age 4 months in a cool, dark place.

(5) Before bottling, add 0.2 grams of sorbate per liter.

Asian Pear

Ingredients
(for making 1 Liter of wine)

- 650 grams of ripe Asian pears
- 700 ml of water
- 450 grams of sugar
- 1 gram of ammonium phosphate
- 1 gram of citric acid
- 0.2 grams of prepared yeast
- 0.2 grams of sulfite
- 0.2 grams of sorbate

The Process

(1) Cut the 650 grams of ripe Asian pears into slices and put in a preparation container.

(2) Add 250 grams of sugar and cover the container with a thick cloth. Let sit for 3 hours. Then add 500 ml of water, 1 gram of citric acid, 1 gram of ammonium phosphate, and the prepared yeast.

(3) Mix and re-cover the container with the thick cloth. Let sit for 5 days.

(4) After 5 days, gently strain and filter into a fermentation container. Heat 200 ml of water and add 200 grams of sugar. Mix well until sugar is dissolved, let cool.

(5) Add to the fermentation container and close with a fermentation stopper. Let sit for 7 days. After 7 days, add 0.2 grams of sulfite to stop the fermentation and let it sit for 10 days.

(6) Drain and age 4 months in a cool, dark place.

(7) Before bottling, add 0.2 grams of sorbate per liter.

Coconut Wine

Ingredients
(for making 1 Liter of wine)

- 300 grams of coconut flakes
- 800 ml of water
- 300 grams of sugar
- 1 gram of citric acid
- 0.2 grams of prepared yeast
- 1 gram of ammonium phosphate
- 0.2 grams of sulfite
- 0.2 grams of sorbate

The Process

(1) In a pot warm the 800 ml of water, add 200 grams of the coconut flakes and stir well. Add 300 grams of sugar and bring the water to a boil, then set it aside and allow to cool. Once cooled, strain the coconut and pour the liquid into a fermentation container.

(2) Add 1 gram of ammonium phosphate, 1 gram of citric acid, and the prepared yeast. Mix and close the fermentation container with a fermentation stopper. Age for 7 days.

(3) Add 0.2 grams of sulfite. 10 days after the fermentation stops, drain. A thin residue of coconut may form on top, leave it. It will sink to the bottom of the container over time.

(4) Age the wine 3 months in a cool, dark place. Before bottling, add 0.2 grams of sorbate per liter. You can either bottle the wine with the sediment or drain it out.

(5) Shake well before drinking.

Longan Wine

Ingredients
(for making 1 Liter of wine)

• 500 grams of longan fruit (pitted)
• 500 ml of water
• 400 grams of sugar
• 1 gram of citric acid
• 1 gram of ammonium phosphate
• 0.2 grams of prepared yeast
• 0.2 grams of sulfite
• 0.2 grams of sorbate

The Process

(1) Peel and remove the pits from all 500 grams of the longan fruit. Put the fruit into a preparation container, add 200 grams of sugar and cover the container with a thick cloth. Let sit for 3 hours.

(2) Add 300 ml of water, 1 gram of ammonium phosphate, 1 gram of citric acid, and the prepared yeast. Mix lightly and re-cover with the thick cloth. Let sit for 3 days.

(3) Strain the liquid into a fermentation container. Heat 200 ml of water and dissolve 200 grams of sugar in it. Let cool, then add to the fermentation container. Close the fermentation container with a fermentation stopper. Let sit for 7 days.

(4) Once fermentation subsides, add 0.2 grams of sulfite and re-seal the container with a fermentation stopper. 10 days after the fermentation stops, drain. Close again with a fermentation stopper. If necessary, drain again until liquid is clear.

(5) Age 4 months in a cool, dark place.

(6) Before bottling, add 0.2 grams of sorbate per liter. Serve cold.

Lucuma Wine

Ingredients
(for making 1 Liter of wine)

• 400 grams of lucuma fruit, pitted
• 700 ml of water
• 300 grams of sugar
• 1 gram of citric acid
• 0.2 grams of prepared yeast
• 1 gram of ammonium phosphate
• 0.2 grams of sulfite
• 0.2 grams of sorbate

The Process

(1) Cut the 400 grams of ripe pitted lucuma fruit into small pieces and put into a preparation container. Sprinkle 150 grams of sugar over the fruit and let sit for 3 hours. Then add 500 ml of water, 1 gram of citric acid, 1 gram of ammonium phosphate, and the prepared yeast. Cover the container with a thick cloth and let sit for 5 days.

(2) Strain and filter into a fermentation container. Heat 200 ml of water and add 150 grams of sugar, mix until the sugar dissolves. Let cool then add to the fermentation container container.

(3) Close the fermentation container with a fermentation stopper and let sit for 7 days. Once fermentation weakens or stops, add 0.2 grams of sulfite.

(4) 10 days after the fermentation has stopped, drain. Drain again if needed to make the liquid clearer. Age 6 months in a cool, dark place.

(5) Before bottling, add 0.2 grams of sorbate per liter.

Noni Wine

Ingredients
(for making 1 Liter of wine)

• 450 grams of chopped noni
• 800 ml of hot water
• 400 grams of sugar
• 1 gram of citric acid
• 1 gram of ammonium phosphate
• 0.2 grams of prepared yeast
• 0.2 grams of sulfite
• 0.2 grams of sorbate

The Process

(1) Rinse and chop the 450 grams of noni and put into a preparation container.

(2) Heat 600 ml of water and add 200 grams of sugar. Stir until the sugar dissolves, then pour over the fruit. Cover the container with a thick cloth and let it sit 4 hours to cool. Then add 1 gram of citric acid, 1 gram of ammonium phosphate, and the prepared yeast. Mix and re-cover the container with the thick cloth. Let sit for 5 days.

(3) Strain and filter into a fermentation container. Heat 200 ml of water and dissolve 200 grams of sugar in it. Allow it to cool before adding it to the fermentation container. Close the fermentation container with a fermentation stopper. Let sit for 7 days.

(4) Once fermentation subsides, add 0.2 grams of sulfite to stop it.

(5) 10 days after fermentation has stopped, drain. Age in a cool, dark place for 6 months.

(6) Before bottling, add 0.2 grams of sorbate per liter.

Papaya Wine

Ingredients
(for making 1 Liter of wine)

- 300 grams of dried papaya
- 5 grams of golden raisins
- 5 grams of cranberries
- 350 grams of sugar
- 800 ml of water
- 1 gram of citric acid
- 1 gram of ammonium phosphate
- 0.2 grams of prepared yeast
- 0.2 grams of sulfite
- 0.2 grams of sorbate

The Process

(1) Bring 600 ml of water to a boil and dissolve 200 grams of sugar in the water. Add 5 grams of golden raisins, 5 grams of cranberries, and 300 grams of dried papaya to a preparation container.

(2) Remove from heat and let cool, cover for 5 hours. Add citric acid, ammonium phosphate, and prepared yeast. Cover with a thick cloth and let sit for 5 days.

(3) Filter into a fermentation container and add 200 ml of water and 150 grams of sugar. Close with a fermentation stopper and let sit for 10 days.

(4) After 10 days have passed, stop the fermentation with 0.2 grams of sulfite.

(5) Drain and age 3 to 4 months in a cool, dark place.

(6) Before bottling, add 0.2 grams of sorbate per liter.

Watermelon Wine

Ingredients
(for making 1 Liter of wine)

- 900 grams of ripe watermelon (the red fleshy part only; no rind)
- 5 grams of thin orange rind
- 200 grams of white sugar
- 300 grams of brown sugar
- 1 gram of citric acid
- 0.2 grams of prepared yeast
- 1 gram of ammonium phosphate
- 0.2 grams of sulfite
- 0.2 grams of sorbate

The Process

(1) Squeeze the 900 grams of watermelon into the preparation container. Add 200 grams of sugar, 5 grams of orange rind, citric acid, and the prepared yeast. Cover the container with a thick cloth and let the brew sit for 5 days.

(2) Strain and filter the brew into a fermentation container tank. Add 300 grams of brown sugar and stir until the sugar dissolves. Close the fermentation container with a fermentation stopper.

(3) Allow to ferment for 7 days, then add 0.2 grams of sulfite to stop the fermentation. Let sit for another 10 days, then drain.

(4) Age 4 months in a cool, dark place.

(5) Before bottling, add 0.2 grams of sorbate per liter.

Melon Wine

Ingredients
(for making 1 Liter of wine)

• 700 grams of ripe melon (without the rind)
• 500 ml of water
• 400 grams of sugar
• 100 grams of golden raisins
• 0.2 grams of prepared yeast
• 1 gram of ammonium phosphate
• 1 gram of citric acid
• 0.2 grams of sulfite
• 0.2 grams of sorbate

The Process

(1) Cut into slices the 700 grams of ripe melon (without the rind) and put into a preparation container. Add 250 grams of sugar and 100 grams of golden raisin. Cover the container with a thick cloth and let sit for 6 hours.

(2) Add 300 ml of water, 1 gram of ammonium phosphate, 1 gram of citric acid, and the prepared yeast to the preparation container. Re-cover the container with the thick cloth and let sit for 5 days.

(3) Heat 200 grams of water in a pot and dissolve 150 grams of sugar in it. Let cool.

(4) Lightly strain and filter the brew into the fermentation container. Add the sugar water and close the container with a fermentation stopper. Allow to ferment for 7 days.

(5) Once fermentation has subsided, add 0.2 grams of sulfite. One week after fermentation has stopped, drain.

(6) Age 3 to 4 months in a cool, dark place.

(7) Before bottling, add 0.2 grams of sorbate per liter.

Vegetable Wines

Vegetable wines can be made from fresh veggies, medicinal herbs, or freshly squeezed or bottled juices.

Carrot Wine

Ingredients
(for making 1 Liter of wine)

- 850 grams of carrots
- 200 ml of water
- 20 grams of thin lemon rind
- 450 grams of sugar
- 600 ml of carrot juice
- 1 gram of citric acid
- 1 gram of ammonium phosphate
- 0.2 grams of prepared yeast
- 0.2 grams of sulfite
- 0.2 grams of sorbate

The Process

(1) Cut the 850 grams of fresh carrots into thin discs and put into a preparation container. Add 200 grams of sugar, 200 ml of water, and 20 grams of lemon rind to the mix. Then add 1 gram of citric acid, 1 gram of ammonium phosphate, and the prepared yeast. Cover the container with a thick cloth and let sit for 5 days.

(2) After 5 days, filter and pour the brew into a fermentation container.

(3) In a separate container, add 600 ml of carrot juice to 250 grams of sugar, stir well. Add to the brew in the fermentation container. Close with a fermentation stopper. Allow the brew to ferment for 7 days.

(4) Once the fermentation subsides, add 0.2 grams of sulfite. 7 days after fermentation has stopped, drain until you get a clear liquid.

(5) Age 4 to 5 months in a cool, dark place.

(6) Before bottling, add 0.2 grams of sorbate per liter.

Beet Wine

Ingredients
(for making 1 Liter of wine)

- 850 ml of beet juice
- 10 grams of lemon rind
- 350 grams of sugar
- 1 gram of ammonium phosphate
- 1 gram of citric acid
- 0.2 grams of prepared yeast
- 0.2 grams of sulfite
- 0.2 grams of sorbate

1 kg of beets produces 460 ml of beet juice

The Process

(1) Put 650 ml of the beet juice into a preparation container. Add 150 grams of sugar and mix well.

(2) Add 10 grams of lemon rind, 1 gram of citric acid, 1 gram of ammonium phosphate, and 0.2 grams of prepared yeast into the preparation container. Stir well and cover the container with a thick cloth. Let sit for 5 days.

(3) Filter the brew into a fermentation container. Add 200 grams of sugar and the remaining 200 ml of beet juice, stir well. Close the fermentation container with a fermentation stopper. Let sit for 7 days.

(4) Once the fermentation calms down or stops, add 0.2 grams of sulfite. Leave for two weeks, then drain.

(5) Age 4 to 5 months in a cool, dark place.

(6) Before bottling, add 0.2 grams of sorbate per liter.

Cherry Tomato

Ingredients
(for making 1 Liter of wine)

- 500 grams of cherry tomatoes
- 20 grams of cranberries
- 700 ml of water
- 200 grams of white sugar
- 300 grams of brown sugar
- 1 gram of citric acid
- 1 gram of ammonium phosphate
- 0.2 grams of prepared yeast
- 0.2 grams of sulfite
- 0.2 grams of sorbate

The Process

(1) Cut each of the 500 grams of ripe cherry tomatoes in half and place in a preparation container. Add 200 grams of white sugar and cover the container with a thick cloth. Let sit for 6 hours. After 6 hours, pour in 400 ml of the water and stir well to dissolve the remaining sugar.

(2) Add 20 grams of cranberries, 1 gram of ammonium phosphate, 1 gram of citric acid, and the prepared yeast to the brew. Re-cover the container with the thick cloth and let sit for 5 days.

(3) Strain the brew and filter into a fermentation container. Heat 200 ml of water and add 300 grams of brown sugar, stir until dissolved and add to the fermentation container. Close the fermentation container with a fermentation stopper and let sit for 8 days.

(4) Once the fermentation subsides, add 0.2 grams of sulfite to stop the fermentation. Wait 14 days then drain as needed until the liquid is clear.

(5) Age 6 months in a cool, dark place.

(6) Before bottling, add 0.2 grams of sorbate per liter.

Potato Wine

Ingredients
(for making 1 Liter of wine)

- 500 grams of white potatoes, rinsed clean
- 800 ml of water
- 450 grams of sugar
- 10 grams of lemon rind
- 1 gram of citric acid
- 1 gram of ammonium phosphate
- 0.2 grams of prepared yeast
- 0.2 grams of sulfite
- 0.2 grams of sorbate
- 1 gram of bentonite

The Process

(1) Cut the 500 grams of potatoes into squares and soak in cold water for an hour. Pour the water out, add clean water and soak again for another hour. Put the potatoes into a pot. Add 600 ml of water to the pot and cook the potatoes on a low flame until softened.

(2) Drain the liquid only into a preparation container. Add 250 grams of sugar and 10 grams of lemon rind. Stir gently and let cool. Once cooled, add 1 gram of ammonium phosphate, 1 gram of citric acid, and the prepared yeast. Cover the container with a thick cloth and let sit for 3 days.

(3) Drain and transfer the liquid into a fermentation container. Dissolve 200 grams of sugar in 200 ml of heated water. Let cool then add to the fermentation container. Close the container with a fermentation stopper and let sit for 7 days.

(4) Once the fermentation subsides, add the sulfite and reseal the container with the fermentation stopper. Let sit for 30 days. After the 30 days, drain. If the brew is too murky, add bentonite as per the instructions on page 15. Once the wine is clear, put it in a cool, dark place and age 4 to 5 months.

(5) Before bottling, add 0.2 grams of sorbate per liter.

Pumpkin Wine

Ingredients
(for making 1 Liter of wine)

• 850 ml of organic pumpkin juice
• 400 grams of sugar
• 1 gram of citric acid
• 0.2 grams of prepared yeast
• 0.2 grams of sulfite
• 0.2 grams of sorbate

The Process

(1) Put 600 ml of the pumpkin juice into a preparation container and add 200 grams of sugar. Then add 1 gram of citric acid, 1 gram of ammonium phosphate, and the prepared yeast. Cover the container with a thick cloth and let sit for 5 days.

(2) Filter the brew into a fermentation container and add the remaining 250 ml of pumpkin juice. Dissolve 200 grams of sugar in hot water and add to the fermentation tank. Close the fermentation container with a fermentation stopper and let sit for 7 days.

(3) After the 7 days had passed, add 0.2 grams of sulfite. Reseal the container and let sit for 30 days, then drain.

(4) Age 6 months in a cool, dark place.

(5) Before bottling, add 0.2 grams of sorbate per liter.

Sweet Potato

Ingredients
(for making 1 Liter of wine)

• 450 grams of sweet potatoes
• 800 ml of water
• 400 grams of sugar
• 0.2 grams of prepared yeast
• 1 gram of citric acid
• 1 gram of ammonium phosphate
• 0.2 grams of sulfite
• 0.2 grams of sorbate

The Process

(1) Rinse 450 grams of sweet potatoes (with the skin on) and put in a pot, pour the water out. Cut the sweet potatoes into squares, put them back in the pot and rinse again. The purpose of rinsing is to reduce or prevent foam buildup during fermentation. Add 400 ml of water to the pot and cook the sweet potatoes until softened. Strain the potatoes and add the liquid alone into a fermentation container. Add 200 grams of sugar (stir until dissolved).

(2) Add the citric acid, ammonium phosphate, and the prepared yeast. Close the fermentation container with a fermentation stopper. Put the container in a sink, since foam may develop and spill over during fermentation. If that happens, open the lid, clean the stopper and close again. Allow the brew to ferment for 5 days. After 5 days, drain.

(3) Heat 400 ml of water and add 200 grams of sugar, stir until the sugar dissolves, let cool. Add the sugar water to the fermentation container and close again with a fermentation stopper. Let sit for 7 days. After 7 days, stop the fermentation with 0.2 grams of sulfite and re-seal the fermentation container with a fermentation stopper.

(4) 10 days after the fermentation stops, drain and close again with a fermentation stopper. Age 4 months in a cool, dark place. Add 0.2 grams of sorbate. 24 hours later, bottle. Before bottling, add 0.2 grams of sorbate per liter.

Onion Wine

Ingredients
(for making 1 Liter of wine)

• 250 grams of peeled red onion (peeled)
• 200 grams of white sugar
• 200 grams of brown sugar
• 800 ml water
• 1 gram of citric acid
• 1 gram ammonium phosphate
• 0.2 grams of yeast
• 0.2 grams of sulfite
• 0.2 grams of sorbate

The Process

(1) Put 250 grams of chopped red onion into the preparation container and add 200 grams of white sugar. Cover with dense cloth for 3 hours.

(2) Add 400 ml of citric acid, ammonium phosphate, 400 ml water and the prepared yeast. Cover with a dense cloth for 5 days.

(3) After 5 days, filter and strain the brew into the fermentation container. Dissolve 200 grams of brown sugar in 400 ml of water and add to the fermentation container. Close with fermentation stopper for 5 days.

(4) After 5 days, add 0.2 grams of sulfite to stop the fermentation. Drain and age for 3 months in a cool and dark place.

(5) Before bottling, add 0.2 grams of sorbate.

Zucchini Wine

Ingredients
(for making 1 Liter of wine)

- 600 grams zucchini (with peel), chopped
- 300 ml water
- 250 ml squeezed zucchini juice
- 400 grams of sugar
- 1 gram citric acid
- 0.2 grams of yeast
- 1 gram ammonium phosphate
- 0.2 grams of sulfite
- 0.2 grams of sorbate

The Process

(1) Cut 600 grams of fresh zucchini (with the rind) into small slices and put into the preparation container. Add 200 grams of sugar and cover with dense cloth for 5 hours.

(2) Add 300 ml water, 1 gram citric acid, 1 gram ammonium phosphate and prepared yeast. Mix and cover with a dense cloth for 5 days. After 5 days filter the brew into a fermentation container.

(3) Add 250 ml of zucchini juice into a pot, add 200 grams of sugar and stir until sugar melts. Add the brew to the fermentation container and close with fermentation stopper for 7 days.

(4) Once fermentation weakens, add 0.2 grams of sulfite. Let sit for 30 days, then strain and drain as needed. Age for 3 to 4 months.

(5) Before bottling, add 0.2 grams of sorbate per liter.

Medicinal Herb Wines

Arugula Wine

Ingredients
(for making 1 Liter of wine)

• 150 grams of arugula
(rinsed and chopped)
• 800 ml of water
• 350 grams of sugar
• 1 gram of citric acid
• 1 gram of ammonium phosphate
• 0.2 grams of prepared yeast
• 0.2 grams of sulfite
• 0.2 grams of sorbate

The Process

(1) Put the 150 grams of freshly chopped arugula into a preparation container. Add 200 grams of sugar and 650 ml of water. Then add 1 gram of citric acid, 1 gram of ammonium phosphate, and the prepared yeast. Cover the container with a thick cloth and let sit for 3 days.

(2) Strain and filter the arugula leaves and transfer the liquid to a fermentation container.

(3) Heat 150 ml of water and add 150 grams of sugar, stir until the sugar is dissolved. Add the sugar water to the fermentation container and close with a fermentation stopper. Let sit for 5 days.

(4) When the fermentation subsides or ends, add 0.2 grams of sulfite.

(5) One week after the fermentation ends, drain and age 4 months in a cool, dark place.

(6) Before bottling, add 0.2 grams of sorbate per liter.

Aloysia Wine

Ingredients
(for making 1 Liter of wine)

- 30 grams of aloysia leaves
- 900 ml of water
- 300 grams of sugar
- 1 gram of ammonium phosphate
- 1 gram of citric acid
- 0.2 grams of prepared yeast
- 0.2 grams of sulfite
- 0.2 grams of sorbate

The Process

(1) Rinse clean the 30 grams of aloysia leaves and put into a preparation container.

(2) In a pot boil 700 ml of the water, add 150 grams of sugar and stir until the sugar dissolves. Pour the sugar water on top of the aloysia leaves, cover the container and let sit for 3 hours to cool.

(3) Strain, filter and pour into a fermentation container. Add the remaining 200 ml of water to the fermentation container and dissolve 150 grams of sugar in it.

(4) Add 1 gram of ammonium phosphate, 1 gram of citric acid, and the prepared yeast. Close the fermentation container with a fermentation stopper and let sit for 7 days.

(5) Once fermentation subsides, add 0.2 grams of sulfite and re-seal the container. 10 days after fermentation has stopped, drain.

(6) Age 3 months in a cool, dark place.

(7) Before bottling, add 0.2 grams of sorbate per liter. Serve cold.

Sage Wine

Ingredients
(for making 1 Liter of wine)

• 20 grams of sage leaves
• 900 ml of water
• 20 grams of lemongrass
• 300 grams of sugar
• 1 gram of citric acid
• 1 gram of ammonium phosphate
• 0.2 grams of prepared yeast
• 0.2 grams of sulfite
• 0.2 grams of sorbate

The Process

(1) Rinse clean the 20 grams of sage leaves and place them in a preparation container, then add 20 grams of lemongrass.

(2) In a pot, boil 600 ml of water and add 150 grams of sugar, stir to dissolve. Pour the sugar water over the sage leaves and allow to sit for 3 hours to cool down.

(3) Gently strain and filter into a fermentation container. Add 1 gram of citric acid, 1 gram of ammonium phosphate, and the prepared yeast. Close the fermentation container with a fermentation stopper and let sit for 5 days. Drain.

(4) Dissolve 150 grams of sugar in 300 ml of water, let cool then add to the fermentation container. Close the container with a fermentation stopper and let sit for 5 days.

(5) Once fermentation has subsided, add 0.2 grams of sulfite, and re-seal the container. Drain as needed until the liquid is clear. Age 3 months in a cool, dark place.

(6) Before bottling, add 0.2 grams of sorbate per liter.

Parsley Wine

Ingredients
(for making 1 Liter of wine)

- 50 grams of fresh parsley leaves
- 20 grams of lemon rind
- 800 ml of water
- 300 grams of sugar
- 1 gram of ammonium phosphate
- 1 gram of citric acid
- 0.2 grams of prepared yeast
- 0.2 grams of sulfite
- 0.2 grams of sorbate

The Process

(1) Rinse clean the parsley leaves and put in a preparation container.

(2) In a pot heat 500 ml of the water and add the 20 grams of lemon rind, boil for 2 minutes. Take out the lemon rind and pour the boiling water over the parsley in the preparation container. Allow to chill in a cool, dark, place for 5 hours.

(3) In a pot, heat 150 ml of water and dissolve 150 grams of sugar in it. Add the sugar water to the preparation container. Add 1 gram of citric acid, 1 gram of ammonium phosphate, and the prepared yeast. Cover the container with a thick cloth and let sit for 5 days.

(4) Filter the brew into a fermentation container. In a pot, dissolve another 150 ml of sugar in 150 ml of water, then add to the fermentation container. Close the fermentation container with a fermentation stopper and let sit for 5 days.

(5) After 5 days, add 0.2 grams of sulfite. 10 days after the fermentation is complete, drain. Age 3 to 4 months in a cool, dark place.

(6) Before bottling, add 0.2 grams of sorbate per liter.

Rosemary Wine

Ingredients
(for making 1 Liter of wine)

• 50 grams of fresh rosemary leaves
• 800 ml water
• 350 grams of sugar
• 15 grams of lemon rind
• 1 gram of ammonium phosphate
• 1 gram of citric acid
• 0.2 grams of prepared yeast
• 0.2 grams of sulfite
• 0.2 grams of sorbate

The Process

(1) Place fresh rosemary leaves into a preparation container. In a pot, boil 400 ml of the water with the 15 grams of lemon rind added for 30 minutes.

(2) Remove the lemon rind and pour the hot liquid over the rosemary leaves in the preparation container. Cover the container with a thick cloth and let the leaves soak for 4 hours.

(3) Add 200 ml of water, 200 grams of sugar, 1 gram of ammonium phosphate, 1 gram of citric acid, and the prepared yeast. Re-cover the container with the thick cloth and let sit for 5 days.

(4) Strain and filter the brew into a fermentation container and add 200 ml water and 150 grams of sugar. Close the fermentation container with a fermentation stopper and let sit for 5 days.

(5) Once the fermentation has weakened, add 0.2 grams of sulfite and re-seal the container with a fermentation stopper.

(6) 10 days after the fermentation has stopped, drain. Age 3 to 4 months in a cool, dark place.

(7) Before bottling, add 0.2 grams of sorbate per liter. Serve cold.

Dill Wine

Ingredients
(for making 1 Liter of wine)

- 150 grams of fresh dill leaves
- 800 ml of water
- 350 grams of sugar
- 10 grams of golden raisins
- 1 gram of citric acid
- 1 gram of ammonium phosphate
- 0.2 grams of prepared yeast
- 0.2 grams of sulfite
- 0.2 grams of sorbate

The Process

(1) In a pot, bring 600 ml of water to a boil and dissolve 200 grams of sugar in it.

(2) Put 150 grams of fresh chopped dill and the 10 grams of golden raisins into a preparation container, add the sugar water and cover for 5 hours.

(3) Add the citric acid, the ammonium phosphate, and the prepared yeast. Re-cover the container with a thick cloth and let sit for 5 days.

(4) Filter the brew into a fermentation container and add 200 ml water and 150 grams of sugar. Close the fermentation container with a fermentation stopper and let sit for 5 days.

(5) Stop fermentation with 0.2 grams of sulfite. Drain and age 3 to 4 months in a cool, dark place.

(6) Before bottling, add 0.2 grams of sorbate per liter. Serve cold.

Damiana Wine

Ingredients
(for making 1 Liter of wine)

- 15 grams of dried damiana
- 900 ml of water
- 200 grams of sugar
- 1 gram of citric acid
- 1 gram of ammonium phosphate
- 0.2 grams of prepared yeast
- 0.2 grams of sulfite
- 0.2 grams of sorbate

The Process

(1) In a pot, bring 800 ml of water to a boil and dissolve in it 100 grams of sugar.

(2) Put the 15 grams of dried damiana leaves into a preparation container. Add the warm sugar water and cover with dense cloth. Let cool for 5 hours.

(3) Filter and transfer the brew into a fermentation container. Then add the citric acid, the ammonium phosphate, and the prepared yeast. Close the fermentation container with a fermentation stopper and let sit for 5 day.

(4) After 5 days, heat 100 ml of water and add 100 grams of sugar, in a pot, until the sugar dissolves. Add the sugar water to the fermentation container and close the container with fermentation stopper. Let sit for 7 days.

(5) When the fermentation weakens or ends, add 0.2 grams of sulfite. One week after the fermentation ends, drain. Age 3 months in a cool, dark place.

(6) Before bottling, add 0.2 grams of sorbate per liter. Serve cold.

White Micromeria

Ingredients
(for making 1 Liter of wine)

- 25 grams of dried white micromeria leaves
- 800 ml of water
- 400 grams of sugar
- 1 gram of citric acid
- 1 gram of ammonium phosphate
- 0.2 grams of prepared yeast
- 0.2 grams of sulfite
- 0.2 grams of sorbate

The Process

(1) In a pot, dissolve 200 grams of sugar in 600 ml of water (bring to a boil). Put the 25 grams of dried white micromeria leaves into a preparation container. Add the sugar water to the preparation container. Cover the container and let sit for 5 hours.

(2) Once cooled, transfer to a fermentation container and add the citric acid, the ammonium phosphate, and the prepared yeast. Close the fermentation container with a fermentation stopper and let sit for 6 days.

(3) In a pot, heat 200 ml of water, add 200 grams of sugar and stir to dissolve. Strain the leaves and add to the fermentation container. Add the sugar water and close the fermentation container with a fermentation stopper. Let sit for 5 days.

(4) When the fermentation weakens or ends, add 0.2 grams of sulfite and let sit for 7 days, then drain.

(5) Age 3 to 4 months in a cool, dark place.

(6) Before bottling, add 0.2 grams of sorbate per liter. Serve cold.

Hawthorn Leaf

Ingredients
(for making 1 Liter of wine)

- 15 grams of hawthorn leaves
- 700 ml of water
- 400 grams of sugar
- 0.2 grams of prepared yeast
- 10 grams of lemon rind
- 1 gram of ammonium phosphate
- 1 gram of citric acid
- 0.2 grams of sulfite
- 0.2 grams of sorbate

The Process

(1) Place the 15 grams of hawthorn leaves into a preparation container and add 10 grams of lemon rind. Boil 300 ml of water, add the leaves and rind. Cover the container and store in a cool, dark place for 4 hours. After 4 hours strain the brew and add to a fermentation container.

(2) In a pot, heat 200 ml of water, and dissolve 200 grams of sugar in it. Let cool, then add to the fermentation container. Add 1 gram of citric acid, 1 gram of ammonium phosphate, and the prepared yeast. Close the fermentation container with a fermentation stopper and let sit for 7 days. Drain.

(3) In a pot, dissolve 200 grams of sugar in 200 ml of warm water. Add the sugar water to the fermentation container and close the container with a fermentation stopper. Let sit for another 5 days.

(4) Once fermentation had subsided, add 0.2 grams of sulfite and re-seal the container with the fermentation stopper. Drain until all the residue is removed. Age 3 months in a cool, dark place.

(5) Before bottling, add 0.2 grams of sorbate per liter.

Melissa Wine

Ingredients
(for making 1 Liter of wine)

- 22 grams of dried melissa officinalis (lemon balm)
- 20 grams of cinnamon sticks
- 20 grams of lemon rind
- 850 ml of water
- 300 grams of brown sugar
- 1 gram of citric acid
- 1 gram of ammonium phosphate
- 0.2 grams of prepared yeast
- 0.2 grams of sulfite
- 0.2 grams of sorbate

The Process

(1) In a pot, dissolve 150 grams of brown sugar in 650 ml of water and bring to boil.

(2) Put into a preparation container the 22 grams of dried melissa officinalis, the 20 grams of cinnamon sticks, and the 20 grams of lemon rind. Add the boiled sugar water and cover the container with a thick cloth. Let cool for 5 hours. Add 1 gram of citric acid, 1 gram of ammonium phosphate, and the prepared yeast to the brew. Re-cover the container with the dense cloth and let sit for 5 days.

(3) After 5 days, filter the brew into a fermentation container and close the container with a fermentation stopper. Let sit for another 5 days.

(4) In a pot, heat 150 ml of water and 150 grams of brown sugar. Mix and allow to cool, then add to the fermentation container. Re-seal the fermentation container with the fermentation stopper. Let sit for 5 days. Once the fermentation weakens or ends, add 0.2 grams of sulfite.

(5) One week (7 days) after fermentation ends, drain. Age 3 to 4 months in a cool, dark place.

(6) Before bottling, add 0.2 grams of sorbate per liter.

Mint Wine

Ingredients
(for making 1 Liter of wine)

- 50 grams of dry mint
- 20 grams of dark raisins
- 850 ml of water
- 250 grams of brown sugar
- 100 grams of white sugar
- 10 grams of lemon rind
- 1 gram of citric acid
- 1 gram of ammonium phosphate
- 0.2 grams of prepared yeast
- 0.2 grams of sulfite
- 0.2 grams of sorbate

The Process

(1) Put the 50 grams of dried mint leaves into a preparation container. In a pot, boil 850 ml of water to dissolve 100 grams of sugar. Add the sugar water to the preparation container along with 20 grams of dark raisins.

(2) Allow the mixture to cool and extract flavors. Once the mixture is cool, add 1 gram of citric acid, 1 gram of ammonium phosphate, and the prepared yeast. Stir well and cover with a thick cloth. Let sit for 5 days.

(3) After 5 days, strain and filter the brew into the fermentation container. In a separate container, add 250 grams of brown sugar to 200 ml water. Stir on a low flame until the sugar dissolves, then add to the fermentation container. Close the fermentation container with a fermentation stopper.

(4) Once the fermentation subsides, add 0.2 grams of sulfite and let sit for 30 days.

(5) Drain as needed. When the liquid is clear, re-seal the fermentation container with the fermentation stopper. Age 5 month in a cool, dark place.

(6) Before bottling, add 0.2 grams of sorbate per liter.

Nettle Wine

Ingredients
(for making 1 Liter of wine)

- 80 grams of dried nettle leaves
- 900 ml water
- 300 grams of sugar
- 10 grams of lemon peel
- 1 gram citric acid
- 1 gram ammonium phosphate
- 0.2 grams of yeast
- 0.2 grams of sulfite
- 0.2 grams of sorbate

The Process

(1) Boil 80 grams of nettle leaves in 800 ml of water. Add 200 grams of sugar and stir until sugar is dissolved. Add the lemon peel and put refrigerate for 30 minutes.

(2) Pour the brew into a preparation container and add 1 gram of citric acid, 1 gram of ammonium phosphate, and the prepared yeast. Stir well and cover with a thick cloth. Let sit for 5 days.

(3) Strain and filter the brew into a fermentation tank. Dissolve 100 grams of sugar in a separate pot with 100 ml of water. Add to the brew and close with fermentation stopper for 5 days.

(4) Once the fermentation subsides, add 0.2 grams of sulfite.

(5) Drain as needed until the liquid is clear, then age in a cool, dark place for 4 months.

(6) Before bottling, add 0.2 grams of sorbate per liter.

Parsley Root

Ingredients
(for making 1 Liter of wine)

- 270 grams fresh parsley root
- 800 ml water
- 400 grams of brown sugar
- 50 grams black raisins
- 2 grams citric acid
- 2 grams of ammonium phosphate
- 0.2 grams of yeast
- 0.2 grams of sulfite
- 0.2 grams of sorbate

The Process

(1) Cut 270 grams of well-rinsed parsley root into thin slices and put in a pot. Add 500 ml of water and boil until root has softened (not too soft, 15 minutes on low heat should do the trick). Let cool and put into the preparation container.

(2) Add 200 grams of brown sugar, 50 grams black raisins, 1 gram ammonium phosphate, 1 gram citric acid, and the prepared yeast. Mix well and cover with a dense cheesecloth for 5 days.

(3) Strain and filter the brew into the fermentation tank. In a separate container, dissolve 200 grams of brown sugar in 300 ml of water, stir until sugar had dissolved, then add into the fermentation container and close with fermentation stopper for 7 days.

(4) Once the fermentation had weakened, add 0.2 grams of sulfite and let sit for 30 days.

(5) Drain as needed until the liquid is clear. Age for 4-5 months.

(6) Before bottling, add 0.2 grams of sorbate.

Cinnamon Wine

Ingredients
(for making 1 Liter of wine)

- 800 ml liters of water
- 30 grams of cinnamon sticks
- 170 grams of white sugar
- 300 grams of brown sugar
- 0.2 grams of prepared yeast
- 1 gram of citric acid
- 1 gram of ammonium phosphate
- 0.2 grams of sulfite
- 0.2 grams of sorbate

The Process

(1) In a pot, bring 500 ml of water to a boil. Add the 30 grams of cinnamon sticks and cook them for 10 minutes on low heat. Cover and put the pot aside. Let cool for 12 hours, then filter the brew into a fermentation container.

(2) In a pot, heat 300 ml of water and dissolve 170 grams of white sugar and 100 grams of brown sugar in it. let cool. Then pour into the fermentation container. Add 1 gram of citric acid, 1 gram of ammonium phosphate, and the prepared yeast. Close the fermentation container with a fermentation stopper and let sit for 7 days.

(3) Drain. Add 200 grams of brown sugar and stir well. Close the fermentation container again with the fermentation stopper. Once the fermentation subsides or stops, add 0.2 grams of sulfite.

(4) After a month, drain as needed. Once the liquid is clear, age 4 months in a cool, dark place.

(5) Before bottling, add 0.2 grams of sorbate per liter.

Green Tea Wine

Ingredients
(for making 1 Liter of wine)

- 18 grams of green tea leaves
- 4 grams of jasmine flowers
- 800 ml water
- 300 grams of sugar
- 1 gram of citric acid
- 1 gram ammonium phosphate
- 0.2 grams of yeast
- 0.2 grams of sorbate
- 0.2 grams of sulfite

The Process

(1) Put the green tea leaves and the jasmin flowers in the preparation container. Dissolve 200 grams of sugar in 700 ml of water and add (without cooling) to the preparation container. Cover and let cool for 5 hours.

(2) Filter the brew into a fermentation tank, then add 1 gram of citric acid, 1 gram of ammonium phosphate, and 0.2 grams of prepared yeast. Close with fermentation stopper for 5 days.

(3) After 5 days, dissolve 100 grams of sugar in 100 ml of water and add to the fermentation tank. Close with the fermentation stopper for 7 days.

(4) Once the fermentation weakens or ends, add 0.2 grams of sulfite. One week later, drain and age for 2 months in a cool and dark place.

(5) Before bottling, add 0.2 grams of sorbate.

Chicory Wine

Ingredients
(for making 1 Liter of wine)

- 140 grams of chopped chicory (also known as curly endive)
- 20 grams of orange rind
- 750 ml of water
- 400 grams of sugar
- 1 gram of citric acid
- 1 gram of ammonium phosphate
- 0.2 grams of prepared yeast
- 0.2 grams of sulfite
- 0.2 grams of sorbate

The Process

(1) In a pot, dissolve 150 grams of sugar in 500 ml of water on a low flame. Add 20 grams of orange rind and let cool.

(2) Put the 140 grams of fresh chopped chicory into a preparation container. Pour in the sugar water and add 1 gram of citric acid, 1 gram of ammonium phosphate, and the prepared yeast. Cover the container with a thick cloth and let sit for 3 days.

(3) Strain and filter the leaves and rind and transfer the liquid to a fermentation container.

(4) In a pot heat 250 ml of water and add 250 grams of sugar. Stir until the sugar dissolves. Add the sugar water to the fermentation container and close the container with a fermentation stopper. Let sit for 7 days.

(5) Once fermentation weakens or ends, add 0.2 grams of sulfite. One week after fermentation ends, drain. Age 4 months in a cool, dark place.

(6) Before bottling, add 0.2 grams of sorbate per liter.

Notes on Wines

In fruit and vegetable wines, once the first fermentation has ended and after draining, check the taste before aging. If the wine is too sweet, then continue to ferment the wine as planned. Otherwise, if the wine is either dry or taste-less, add sugar before aging. Keep in mind that adding sugar can lower the percentage of alcohol in the wine. Different wines could result in the fruit or the foam overflowing. So pay attention. It is recommended you keep the container in the sink to lower the foam and push the fruit down. If you leave the container in there for a couple of hours it should be fine. When ferment-ing fruit wines, it's recommended to stir the fruit at least once a day.

Base: Every liqueur needs an alcoholic base, it can be 40% vodka or 40% brandy.

Sweetener: Liqueurs can be sweetened with either sugar or honey.
Seasoning: Spice up liqueurs with either sweet spices or honey.

* * * * *

There are two primary ways to make liqueurs: the Hot Method and the Cold Method.

The Hot Method is especially good for liqueurs made with spices, herbs, and medicinal plants. First wash the plants, boil them, and then let them cool. Filter and add the alcohol.

The Cold Method is particularly useful when making liqueurs from fruits and sweet vegetables. Put a piece of fruit into a jar, add alcohol and let soak for a number of days, weeks or months (depending on the recipe). Then add sugar and water. Quantities will vary, again depending on the recipe. You can soak whole or sliced fruits in the alcohol. When soaking whole fruits, you'll get a clearer liqueur but a less aggressive taste. The most delicious liqueurs aren't clear, and they have a higher degree of sedimentation at the bottom of the jar.

The quantities in the recipes herein are calculated per 1 liter.
When I write "vodka" I mean a 40% vodka.

Apple & Honey

Ingredients
(for making 1 Liter of liqueur)

• 300 ml of organic apple juice
• 100 ml of water
• 120 grams of sugar
• 100 grams of honey
• 580 ml of vodka

The Process

(1) In a pot, heat 100 ml of water and add 120 grams of sugar. Stir to dissolve the sugar. Let cool.

(2) Add 100 grams of honey (pour slowly) and mix until the honey and sugar have dissolved.

(3) Add 300 ml of apple juice, and continue to mix until a uniform texture is formed. Cover the pot and store in a cool, dark place for 2 hours.

(4) Add 580 ml of vodka and mix gently. Put into an airtight container and let sit for 24 hours in a cool, dark place. Serve cold.

Apple Cinnamon

Ingredients
(for making 1 Liter of liqueur)

• 200 ml organic apple juice
• 200 ml of water
• 200 grams of sugar
• 30 grams of cinnamon sticks
• 530 ml of vodka

The Process

(1) Rinse the 30 grams of cinnamon sticks and place into a preparation container.

(2) In a pot, heat 200 ml of water and pour onto the cinnamon sticks in the preparation container. Close the preparation container with a lid and leave for 5 hours to cool.

(3) Strain the cinnamon and the liquid into an airtight glass container and close with a lid.

(4) In a separate pot, pour 200 ml of organic apple juice and 200 grams of sugar. Mix then add to the cinnamon extract in the glass container.

(5) Add 530 ml of vodka and gently mix. Seal the glass container with a lid and keep in a cool, dark place for 24 hours. Serve cold

Mocha liqueur

Ingredients
(for making 1 Liter of liqueur)

- 35 grams of mocha coffee
- 580 ml of vodka
- 270 grams of sugar
- 280 ml of water
- 2 ml of organic vanilla extract

The Process

(1) In a metal pot, heat 280 ml of water. In a small bowl, mix 270 grams of sugar and 35 grams of mocha coffee.

(2) Add the sugar and mocha mix to the hot water, stir well until a uniform texture is formed.

(3) Heat on low flame until the brew begins to boil, then add the organic vanilla. Stir and remove from the flame. Put aside and let cool for 30 minutes.

(4) Refrigerate the brew overnight (whatever foam was formed will disappear).

(5) Add 580 ml of vodka to the mixture and stir well. Put into an air-tight container.

(6) Age for 48 hours before bottling.

Pomegranate

Ingredients
(for making 1 Liter of liqueur)

- 400 grams of pomegranate arils
- 10 grams of dark raisins
- 300 grams of sugar
- 100 ml of pomegranate juice
- 520 ml of vodka

The Process

(1) Put the 400 grams of pomegranate arils into a preparation container. Add 200 grams of sugar and 10 grams of dark raisins. Stir to disperse the sugar and cover the container with a thick cloth.

(2) Let sit for 12 hours then store in a cool, dark place for 24 hours.

(3) Strain and filter the clear liquid into a clean container (without the precipitate).

(4) Add 100 ml of pomegranate juice and dissolve 100 grams of sugar in it. Total liquid will be approximately 600 ml.

(5) Drain into a clean container to remove all sediment.

(6) Add 520 ml of vodka to the container, stir well and close the lid. Let sit for 48 hours.

(7) Age for 48 hours before bottling.

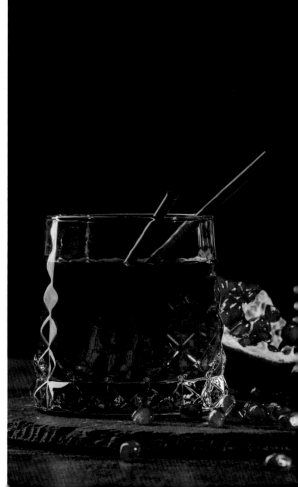

Asian Pear

Ingredients
(for making 1 Liter of liqueur)

- 400 grams of Asian pears (Nashi)
- 530 ml of vodka
- 400 ml of water
- 200 grams of sugar

The Process

(1) Rinse the 400 grams of Asian pears (Nashi) and place in a glass jar.

(2) Add 530 ml of vodka. Close the jar with a tight-sealed lid and put in a cool, dark, place for 14 days.

(3) In a pot, heat 400 ml of water and add 200 grams of sugar. Stir well until the sugar is dissolved and let cool.

(4) Filter the pears into a new, air-tight container and add the sugar water.

(5) Seal the container with a lid and let sit for 48 hours.

Marlua Fruit

Ingredients
(for making 1 Liter of liqueur)

• 400 grams of peeled marlua
• 300 ml of water
• 230 grams of sugar
• 600 ml of vodka

The Process

(1) Put the 400 grams of peeled marlua into a sealed container. Add 600 ml of vodka and seal closed with a lid.

(2) Place the container in a cool, dark place and let sit for 3 weeks.

(3) In a pot, heat 300 ml of water, add 230 grams of sugar and stir until the sugar is dissolved. Let cool.

(4) Strain the marlua into a new container and add the sugar water.

(5) Bottle and age 48 hours in a cool, dark place.

Loquat Liqueur

Ingredients
(for making 1 Liter of liqueur)

• 180 grams pitted loquats
(after washing and drying)
• 410 ml water
• 200 grams of sugar
• 700 ml vodka

The Process

(1) Bring 300 ml water to a boil and add the loquats, boil for 2 minutes and then refrigerate for 30 minutes.

(2) Pour the brew into a jar and add 700 ml of vodka, and seal, let sit in a dark and cool place for 30 days.

(3) Preheat 110 ml of water, add 200 grams of sugar, stir to dissolve and let cool.

(4) Add the sugar water to the brew and mix well.

(5) Bottle and let sit in a cool and dark place for 48 hours. Serve cold.

Date Liqueur

Ingredients
(for making 1 Liter of liqueur)

• 240 grams of date honey
• 460 ml of vodka
• 270 ml of hot water
• 130 grams of sugar
• 1 ml of organic vanilla extract

The Process

(1) In a small saucepan, heat 270 ml of water and dissolve 130 grams of sugar in it.

(2) Remove the pan from the flame and let cool.

(3) When the water is slightly warm, slowly add the 240 grams of date honey to the water, stirring as you add them.

(4) Cover the pan with a lid and let sit for 48 hours.

(5) Slowly add 460 ml of vodka while stirring, and seal in a glass container.

(6) Let sit for 48 hours in a cool, dark place.

(7) Pour into bottles and serve cold.

Gooseberry

Ingredients
(for making 1 Liter of liqueur)

• 400 grams of sweet, ripe goose-berries
• 660 ml of vodka, 40%
• 220 ml of water
• 280 grams of sugar

The Process

(1) Put the 400 grams of ripe gooseberries into a glass jar and add 660 ml of vodka.

(2) Close the jar with a lid and place in a cool, dark place for 21 days.

(3) In a pot heat 220 ml of water and add 280 grams of sugar. Stir well and let cool.

(4) Filter the brew into a new hermetic jar, add the sugar water and seal closed.

(5) Put aside in a cool, dark place for 48 hours.

(6) Pour into bottles and serve cold.

Honey Cinnamon

Ingredients
(for making 1 Liter of liqueur)

- 30 grams of cinnamon sticks
- 200 ml of water
- 120 grams of sugar
- 120 grams of honey
- 540 ml of vodka

The Process

(1) Rinse clean the 30 grams of cinnamon sticks, then break them into pieces and put into a pot. Add the 200 ml of water, 120 grams of sugar, and honey. Bring to a boil for 2 minutes. Stir well until a uniform texture is formed.

(2) Cover the pot and let sit 4 hours to cool.

(3) Remove the cinnamon sticks and strain the liquid into a new hermetic jar.

(4) Add 540 ml of vodka and stir. Seal the jar closed and let sit for 48 hours in a cool, dark place.

(5) Pour into a bottle and serve cold.

Kumquat Liqueur

Ingredients
(for making 1 Liter of liqueur)

• 300 grams of ripe kumquats
• 700 ml of vodka, 40%
• 200 grams of sugar
• 400 ml of water

The Process

(1) Rinse clean the 300 grams of kumquats and put inside an air-tight jar. Add 700 ml of vodka, put the lid on the jar, and seal the jar closed.

(2) Let sit 3-4 weeks in a cool, dark place.

(3) Strain the fruit and pour the kumquat juice into a bottle and seal the bottle.

(4) In a pot, heat the 400 ml of water and add the 200 grams of sugar. Stir and let cool.

(5) Pour the cooled sugar water into the preparation container.

(6) Using a strainer, gently add the kumquat juice to the preparation container. Mix and close the container.

(7) Let sit for 48 hours in a cool, dark place.

Lychee Liqueur

Ingredients
(for making 1 Liter of liqueur)

- 450 grams of peeled lychee (without the kernel)
- 500 ml of vodka, 40%
- 370 ml of water
- 250 grams of sugar

The Process

(1) Put the 450 grams of the seedless lychee into a glass, airtight jar. Add 500 ml of vodka and seal the jar closed. Store in a cool, dark place for 21 days.

(2) Filter the contents of the jar into a bottle and seal the bottle closed with a lid. Put aside for 21 days.

(3) In a pot, heat the 370 ml water and add the 250 grams of sugar. Stir to dissolve the sugar.

(4) Put the sugar water in a clean jar and let cool. Once cooled, add the contents of the bottle to the jar, stir well and seal the jar.

(5) Let sit for 48 hours in a cool, dark place. Bottle the liqueur and put in the fridge.

Serve cold.

Honey Liqueur

Ingredients
(for making 1 Liter of liqueur)

• 260 grams of honey
• 80 grams of sugar
• 280 ml of water
• 480 ml of vodka, 40%
• 1 ml of organic vanilla extract
• 4 ml of brandy, 40%

The Process

(1) In a pot, heat the 280 ml of water, add the 80 grams of sugar and the 260 grams of honey. Mix well until you get a uniform texture.

(2) Cover the pot with a thick cloth and allow to cool down.

(3) Add 1 ml of organic vanilla extract, 4 ml of brandy, and 480 ml of vodka. Mix well.

(4) Pour into a bottle and age for a month in a dark, cool place.

Carob Liqueur

Ingredients
(for making 1 Liter of liqueur)

- 160 grams of raw carob honey
- 350 ml of water
- 4 ml of brandy
- 480 ml of vodka
- 80 grams of sugar

The Process

(1) In a pot, heat 350 ml of water. Add the 80 grams of sugar and the 160 grams of carob honey. Allow to cool.

(2) Add the 4 ml of brandy and the 480 ml of vodka to the mix and stir well.

(3) Pour into a bottle and seal.

(4) Age 1 month in a cool, dark place.

Lemonade Liqueur

Ingredients
(for making 1 Liter of liqueur)

• 130 grams lemon peel
• 40 grams of orange peel
• 700 ml Vodka 40%
• 280 ml water
• 200 grams of sugar

The Process

(1) Add the lemon peel and orange peel into a hermetic glass container and add 700 ml vodka.

(2) Close the lid tightly and place in a cool, dark place for 14 days.

(3) Heat 280 ml of water and dissolve 200 grams of sugar and let cool.

(4) Filter the peels and add to the brew.

(5) Fill bottles to seal and sleep 48 hours.

Cinnamon Liqueur

Ingredients
(for making 1 Liter of liqueur)

• 30 grams of cinnamon sticks
• 500 ml of vodka, 40%
• 460 ml of water
• 180 grams of sugar

The Process

(1) Break 30 grams of the cinnamon sticks into pieces and put into a glass jar with an air-tight lid.

(2) Add the 500 ml of vodka to the jar.

(3) Seal the jar and store in a cool, dark place for 14 days.

(4) In a pot, dissolve the 180 grams of sugar in 460 ml of hot water. Let cool.

(5) Strain the cinnamon sticks and add the juice to the sugar water. Stir well.

(6) Pour into a bottle and seal. Age 48 hours in a cool, dark place.

Wumpa Liqueur

Ingredients
(for making 1 Liter of liqueur)

• 400 grams wumpa fruit
• 510 ml vodka
• 370 ml water
• 200 grams of sugar

The Process

(1) Put 400 grams of wumpa fruit into a glass jar, add 510 ml of vodka. Close the lid and place in a dark, cool place for 21 days.

(2) Heat 370 ml of water and add 200 grams of sugar, mix until the sugar dissolves and let cool.

(3) Filter and strain the wumpa juice into a clean container and add the sugared water.

(4) Seal hermetically in a glass container for 48 hours.

Acai Liqueur

Ingredients
(for making 1 Liter of liqueur)

• 300 grams of acai fruit
• 300 grams of sugar
• 320 ml water
• 20 grams of blueberries
• 520 ml vodka

The Process

(1) Put 300 grams of acai fruit into a glass jar, add 20 grams of blueberry, and 520 ml vodka.

(2) Seal hermetically and store in a dark and cool place for 21 days.

(3) Heat 320 ml of water and add 300 grams of sugar, stir until sugar had dissolved and let cool.

(4) Strain the contents of the brew into a new jar, add the sugared water and mix well.

(5) Seal the jar and let sit for 48 hours. Bottle and serve cold.

Babaco Liqueur

Ingredients
(for making 1 Liter of liqueur)

• 300 grams babaco fruit, peeled
• 420 ml vodka
• 400 ml water
• 300 grams of sugar

The Process

(1) Put 300 grams of babaco fruit in a glass jar and add 420 ml of vodka.

(2) Close the lid and place in a dark, cool place for 21 days.

(3) Heat 400 ml of water and add 300 grams of sugar, stir until sugar had dissolved and let cool.

(4) Filter the babaco brew into a new glass container and add the sugared water.

(5) Seal hermetically for 48 hours.

Rambutan Liquor

Ingredients
(for making 1 Liter of liqueur)

• 500 grams of rambutan
• 350 ml water
• 250 grams of sugar
• 500 ml vodka

The Process

(1) Peel 500 grams of rambutan, remove the kernel and cut each fruit into four equal pieces.

(2) Place inside a clean jar. Make sure it's clear of any left-over peel or seeds (they're toxic!).

(3) Add 500 ml vodka 40% and seal the jar. Store in a dark, cool place for 21 days.

(4) Heat 350 ml of water and add 250 grams of sugar, stir until the sugar had dissolved.

(5) Put the sugared water into a clean container and let cool.

(6) Once cooled, filter the rambutan brew into the cooled sugar water, mix and seal hermetically.

(7) Let it sit 48 hours. Bottle and serve cold.

Java Plum

Ingredients
(for making 1 Liter of liqueur)

• 250 grams of java plum fruit
• 470 ml vodka
• 350 ml water
• 280 grams of sugar

The Process

(1) Put 250 grams of java plum fruit inside a glass jar, then add 470 ml of vodka.

(2) Close the lid and place in a dark, cool place for 21 days.

(3) Heat 350 ml of water and add 280 grams of sugar, mix until the sugar had dissolved and let cool.

(4) Filter the fruity brew into a clean container, then add the sugared water.

(5) Seal hermetically for 48 hours.

Fig liqueur

Ingredients
(for making 1 Liter of liqueur)

• 600 grams of ripe figs
• 150 grams of sugar
• 280 ml water
• 700 ml vodka

The Process

(1) Slice figs in half and put into glass container, add 700 ml of vodka and seal.

(2) Let it sit in a cold and dark place for 14 days.

(3) Preheat 280 ml of water and add 150 grams of sugar, stir until the sugar had dissolved and let cool.

(4) Once sugared water had cooled, pour into the fruity brew, mix well.

(5) Bottle and seal. Put away in a dark place for 48 hours.

Chocolate Mint

Ingredients
(for making 1 Liter of liqueur)

• 350 ml of water
• 350 grams sugar
• 35 grams of cocoa powder
• 6 ml of organic vanilla extract
• 50 grams of dried mint leaves
• 10 grams of mocha coffee
• 490 ml vodka

The Process

(1) Put 350 gram of sugar into a small container, add 35 grams of cocoa powder, 10 grams of instant mocha coffee and mix well.

(2) In a separate container, heat 350 ml of water. Add 50 grams of dried mint leaves, boil for 5 minutes on low fire.

(3) Remove from the heat and allow to cool for an hour.

(4) Filter the minty liquid and squeeze the leaves, transfer the liquid to a pot and put back on low flame, bring to boil.

(5) Pour the coffee mixture (1) into the pot and stir well until a uniform texture is obtained. Leave to cool.

(6) Add 490 ml of vodka to the brew and mix.

(7) Pour into bottles and leave in a dark and cool place for 48 hours. Serve cold

Cocoa Liqueur

Ingredients
(for making 1 Liter of liqueur)

- 220 grams of sugar
- 30 grams of cocoa powder
- 100 grams of chocolate powder
- 470 ml of water
- 5 ml organic vanilla extract
- 350 ml of vodka

The Process

(1) Put 220 grams of sugar in a container. Add 30 grams of cocoa powder, 100 grams of chocolate powder, stir well and set aside.

(2) In a small pot, heat 470 ml of water and add the mixture to the sugar mixture.

(3) Add 5 ml of vanilla extract, mix well until a uniform texture is obtained and leave to cool.

(4) Add 350 ml of vodka and mix well.

(5) Place in a dark and cool place for 48 hours.

Dried Fruit Liqueurs

Please wash dry fruit well before adding them to the brew.

Pineapple Liqueur

Ingredients
(for making 1 Liter of liqueur)

- 130 grams of dry pineapple
- 260 ml vodka 40%
- 120 grams of sugar
- 130 ml water

The Process

(1) Put dry pineapple into a hermetic jar and add 260 ml vodka, seal and keep in a dark and cool place for 14 days.

(2) Heat 130 ml water and add 120 grams of sugar, stir until the sugar had dissolved and refrigerate for 30 minutes.

(3) Strain and filter the pineapple brew into a hermetically-sealed jar.

(4) Add the sugared water and mix well.

(5) Bottle and place in a cool place for 48 hours. Serve cold.

Coconut Caramel

Ingredients
(for making 1 Liter of liqueur)

- 70 grams of dried coconut
- 30 grams of dried caramel
- 600 ml vodka 40%
- 280 grams of sugar
- 300 ml water

The Process

(1) Put the coconut and caramel in a hermetic glass jar, add the 600 ml vodka and seal the jar.

(2) Put away for 3 weeks in a dark and cool place.

(3) Heat 300 ml water and add 280 grams of sugar, stir until the sugar had dissolved and let cool.

(4) Strain the brew into the jar with the sugared water and mix well.

(5) Let cool for 48 hours.

Anise Liqueur

Ingredients
(for making 1 Liter of liqueur)

- 100 grams of anise stars
- 800 ml vodka 40%
- 170 grams of sugar
- 160 ml water

The Process

(1) Add 100 grams of anise stars into a sealed glass jar. Add 800 ml vodka and close with a hermetic seal for 3 weeks.

(2) Heat 160 ml of water and add 170 grams of sugar, stir until sugar had dissolved and let cool.

(3) Filter the anise brew into the sugared water.

(4) Stir well. Bottle and let sit for 48 hours before drinking.

Mango Liqueur

Ingredients
(for making 1 Liter of liqueur)

- 160 grams of dried mango
- 500 ml vodka 40%
- 180 grams of sugar
- 280 ml water

The Process

(1) Slice each dry mango into 3 or 4 small pieces, put the dry fruit into a clean, hermetic jar.

(2) Add 500 ml vodka. Seal the jar and keep in a dark, cold place for 21 days.

(3) Dissolve the sugar in 280 ml water, let cool.

(4) Filter the mango brew into a clean and sanitized hermetic container, add the sugared water into the container and mix.

(5) Bottle and place in a cool place for 48 hours. Serve cold.

Apricot

Ingredients
(for making 1 Liter of liqueur)

- 400 grams dry apricot
- 5 grams black raisin
- 300 ml water
- 230 grams of sugar
- 600 ml vodka

The Process

(1) Add the dry apricots and black raisins into a hermetic jar.

(2) Add 600 ml of vodka and seal.

(3) Put away in a dark and cool place for 21 days.

(4) Heat 300 ml of water, add 230 grams of sugar and stir until the sugar had dissolved. Let cool.

(5) Strain the apricot juice into the container and mix with the sugar water.

(6) Bottle and age for 48 hours before serving. Serve cold.

Apple

Ingredients
(for making 1 Liter of liqueur)

• 160 grams of dried apple
• 500 ml Vodka
• 170 grams of white sugar
• 60 grams of brown sugar
• 360 ml water

The Process

(1) Put 160 grams of dry apple into a hermetic jar and add 500 ml of vodka.

(2) Seal and keep in a dark and cold place for 14 days.

(3) Heat 360 ml of water and add 170 grams of white sugar, and 60 grams of brown sugar. Stir until the sugar had dissolved and let cool.

(4) Strain the apples into a hermetic jar.

(5) Add the water and sugar mixture and mix well.

(6) Place in a dark and cool place for 48 hours. Serve cold.

Goji Berry

Ingredients
(for making 1 Liter of liqueur)

• 250 grams of goji berry
• 460 ml vodka 40%
• 260 grams of sugar
• 400 ml water

The Process

(1) Put 250 grams of dry goji berry into a clean hermetic jar. Add 460 ml vodka.

(2) Seal the jar and keep in a dark, cold place for 21 days.

(3) Preheat 400 ml of water and add 260 grams of sugar, stir until the sugar had dissolved, let cool.

(4) Strain the fruit into a clean, sanitized container.

(5) Add the sugared water and mix. Put in bottles and place in a cool place for 48 hours.

Spicy Ginger

Ingredients
(for making 1 Liter of liqueur)

- 250 grams grated ginger
- 500 ml vodka
- 370 ml water
- 200 grams of sugar

The Process

(1) Soak 250 grams of ginger in water overnight.

(2) In the morning, filter out the water and chop the ginger into small, fine pieces (or use a grater).

(3) Place the ginger in a clean hermetic jar. Add 500 ml of vodka, seal and put away for 10 days.

(4) After 10 days, strain the ginger juice into a clean, hermetic jar.

(5) Heat 370 ml of water and add 200 grams of sugar, mix until the sugar had dissolved. Add to the ginger brew, mix well and seal, let sit for 48 hours.

(6) Filter into bottles with a sieve. Serving at room temperature is recommended.

"Xanax" Liqueur

A magical concoction that'll keep your mind at ease. No Xanax needed!

Ingredients

- 10 grams of shredded coconut
- 3 grams of lavender
- 5 grams of ginger
- 5 grams of damiana leaves
- 5 grams of chamomile
- 3 grams melissa leaves
- 430 ml vodka
- 400 ml water
- 280 grams of sugar

The Process

(1) Wash the leaves well and place in a clean glass jar, add 430 ml of vodka and seal the jar.

(2) Place in a dark and cool place for 14 days.

(3) Gently strain the leaves and filter into a clean jar.

(4) Heat 400 ml water and add 280 grams of sugar, stir until the sugar dissolves.

(5) Let cool and add to the brew, mix well and bottle.

(6) Place the bottle in a dark and cool place for 48 hours before use.

Fruit Punch

Ingredients
(for making 1 Liter of liqueur)

- 100 grams of cherries
- 100 grams of blueberries
- 80 grams of strawberry
- 80 grams of blackberry
- 400 ml water
- 200 grams of sugar
- 480 ml vodka

The Process

(1) Put all the fruit into a hermetic container, add 480 ml of vodka.

(2) Seal hermetically for 30 days.

(3) Strain the fruits and pour the liquid into a clean jar.

(4) Dissolve 200 grams of sugar in 400 ml of water, let cool and mix into the brew.

(5) Seal and let sit for 48 hours.

Medicinal Plant Liqueur

Mint Liqueur

Ingredients
(for making 1 Liter of liqueur)

- 30 grams of mint leaves
- 420 ml water
- 170 grams of brown sugar
- 460 ml of vodka

The Process

(1) Rinse the mint leaves and place in a heat-resistant container.

(2) In a pot, add 420 ml of water and bring to a boil on a low flame, add 170 grams of brown sugar and stir until the sugar had dissolved.

(3) Pour the sugared water onto the mint leaves and leave for two hours.

(4) Once the brew has cooled, strain the liquid into a separate container and add 460 ml of vodka.

(5) Stir well and bottle.

(6) Bottles should be kept in a cool and dark place for 48 hours before consumption. Serve cold.

Dried Chamomile

Ingredients
(for making 1 Liter of liqueur)

• 25 grams of dried chamomile flowers
• 480 ml vodka 40%
• 280 grams of sugar
• 350 ml water

The Process

(1) Put 25 grams of dried chamomile flowers in a hermetic glass jar. Add 480 ml vodka and seal.

(2) Put away in a dark and cool place for 14 days.

(3) Strain into a new glass container.

(4) Dissolve 280 grams of water in 350 ml of water, stir and let cool, then add to the brew. Mix well and seal for 48 hours.

(5) Gently strain and pour into bottles.

Serve cold.

Liquid Stevia

Just a pure alcoholic sweetener to give some kick to your morning's coffee!

Ingredients

- 35 grams of washed stevia leaves
- 350 ml water
- 150 ml vodka

The Process

(1) Put 35 grams of stevia leaves into a heat-resistant preparation container.

(2) Bring 350 ml of water to a boil and pour on the leaves.

(3) Cover and keep in a cool place for 5 hours.

(4) After 5 hours, strain the brew into a new hermetically-sealed container and 150 ml of vodka.

(5) Seal for 24 hours.

Spicy Pepper

Ingredients
(for making 1 Liter of liqueur)

• 350 ml vodka 40%
• 5 spicy serrano peppers (including kernels). You can also use habanero at your own risk.

The Process

(1) Place the peppers inside a glass jar, add 350 ml vodka.

(2) Cover and keep in a dark and cool place for 14 days.

(3) Pour the brew and the peppers into a bottle and seal for 24 hours.

(4) Serve cold.